JUST SAY A FEW WORDS

THE COMPLETE SPEAKER'S HANDBOOK

BOB MONKHOUSE

Illustrations by Ian Dicks

In a recent public survey about fear, it was discovered that more people feared the prospect of having to stand up and speak to an audience than feared dying. If you're one of those people who are more frightened of speaking in public than you are of disease, bankruptcy or a visit from your mother-in-law, then this book is for you.

In this volume, the award-winning Toastmaster Bob Monkhouse guides you through the simple steps that will make you a confident and effective speaker. Whether you need to address a business meeting, propose a toast at your daughter's wedding, or speak to any group of unnervingly attentive faces with "just a few words," this seasoned professional tells you exactly how to do it.

How to begin a speech is a subject that deserves several interesting approaches and gets them here. Bob Monkhouse does not neg-

(Continued on back flap)

JUST SAY A FEW WORDS

JUST SAY A FEW WORDS

THE COMPLETE SPEAKER'S HANDBOOK

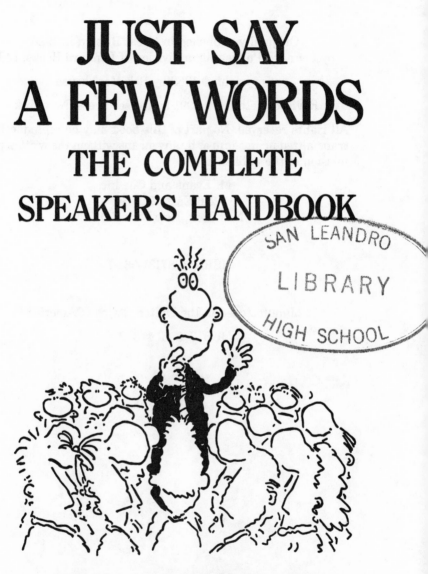

BOB MONKHOUSE

M. Evans and Company, Inc.   New York

Originally published in Great Britain in 1988
by Lennard Publishing, a division of Lennard Books, Ltd.

Copyright © 1988 by Bob Monkhouse

Revised material © 1991 by Dorset Press, New York

M. Evans and Co., Inc.
216 East 49th St.
New York, New York 10017

ISBN: 0-87131-661-7

Manufactured in the United States of America

9 8 7 6 5 4 3 2

Contents

The Androcles Effect

Androcles faced the most terrifying of man-eating lions ever to enter an ancient Roman Colosseum. But the gentle fellow had a way of taming the ferocious beast. He simply whispered into its ear and it abandoned all thought of eating him. Summoned to the royal box, Androcles was asked his secret by the emperor.

"It's this, my lord. I merely tell the lion that, as soon as he's finished dinner, he'll be asked to say a few words."

If Androcles has whispered in your ear, my friend, let the next few pages help to restore your lion's courage.

Introduction

In a recent public survey about fears, which do you suppose people were more afraid of—speaking in public or dying?

That's right. More people feared the prospect of having to stand up and speak to an audience than feared dying. I've done both at the same time and that's even worse. So, if you're one of those people who have said that they're more frightened of making a speech than they are of disease, bankruptcy or a mother-in-law's visit, then I can help you.

With this book as your guide you can learn the simple steps that will help you become a confident and effective speaker. Read it and you will find out how to overcome nervousness and make your tension work for you. Follow my techniques and you will find that few means of communication are as rewarding as public speaking. And the learning process is fun.

Hosting a talk show is the oddest activity in television. I once heard it described as "two consenting adults performing an unnatural act in public". Well, making a speech isn't a natural activity. It's a performance, a show, a piece of artifice that needs the right sort of preparation, polish and practice. There's no lazy way—but I can show you short cuts and tricks of the trade that you'll enjoy using.

This is not a book for veteran professional speakers, although even those intrepid warhorses will find many new insights and tips. There's also a fund of fresh one-liners and modernized classics of humor never published before. What's more, I've tested the worth of every one of them in many a banqueting hall and ballroom before recommending them here, so you don't have to wade through a lot of duds.

I have written this guide for those private people who are required, just occasionally, to rise before a wedding party, a club meeting, a business gathering, or any cluster of unnervingly attentive faces to "say a few words". I've kept it simple and chatty because that is the language of easy communication. And easy communication is what speech-giving is all about.

We'll begin with basic stuff, ways to focus your thoughts and gather ideas. Then we'll explore ways of constructing a speech, assessing the audience's needs, and projecting your most effective image from entrance to exit. The pace of instruction is up to you.

Special sections examine the deadpan delivery of humor, how to let your ideas grow, and the best uses of triviality to emphasize your most serious messages. How to begin a speech is a subject which deserves several interesting approaches and gets them, likewise the ways in which you can construct the middle and end of what you want to say.

There are dozens more fascinating aspects of public speaking that we'll analyze along the way—but enough about the menu, let's get to the meal. Or, rather, let's get to the deal.

My Promise To You

I'll demonstrate every method I know of creating an amusing and informative speech. I'll explain the secrets of performance techniques, how to simulate spontaneity, plus your impact on your audience, and command their attention. Together we can establish a set of ground rules in your mind that will enable you to deal with any situation that calls upon you to speak to a group of humans, whether they're your family, sales force, voters, a bunch of kids, a debating society, shop-floor workers, boardroom directors, monks, drunks, punks, academicians, statisticians, rag-trade philosophers, newspaper cynics, pundits, bandits, cops, fops, chums, bums, or twenty-six million viewers. But in exchange for whatever I can give you, you have to promise me something,

Your Commitment To Me

Give me your time and your mind. Be patient with me. Join me wholeheartedly in this endeavor and it will pay greater dividends than you can imagine in the years to come. You'll be surprised how much pleasure and fulfillment are to be had from speaking well in public. And applause is a terrific reward. Just ask the man who gets it.

And keep this book somewhere you can easily find it. Stash it in the john if you like. But please, don't use its pages for any purpose other than reference—and recording. Oh yes, there's space at the back for you to add your own notes. This is going to be one of those joint-authorship jobs. Let's both pull our weight, right?

First Steps

If, say, you are a businessman used to corporate terms you may feel the language of entertainment is unsuitable for your kind of public speaking. You employ financial, industrial and commercial idioms, and that is the language you are comfortable with.

True, but at the very moment you rise to talk to an audience, you also step onto the stage. When you open your mouth to speak, you enter show business. The more you can accept that, the more successful you will be.

Today people have become pretty sophisticated about what entertains them and what does not. The old magic and mystery of the theater no longer create wonder along with amusement. The public knows how the tricks are done and its patience with an unsatisfactory performance has grown short. Sometimes I've suspected entire theater audiences of holding imaginary remote controls with their thumbs on the off-button. Merely to gain and hold their attention requires showmanship. But this is something that can be acquired.

MAKE IT SOUND GOOD

I am sure you know of some executive who is sought after as a speaker because he has learned to make himself impressive. His audience may know next to nothing about his firm, the American Stuff Manufacturing Co. Inc., but when this fellow starts talking, they listen. He's confident, he's informative, and everyone can understand each point he makes. He keeps them interested in what he's going to say next and, every now and then, he scores a comfortable laugh. When he sits down, that audience will regard the American Stuff Manufacturing Co. Inc. differently. The firm and what it does will have become a familiar and friendlier part of life.

This is fact, not fancy. Every accomplished communicator in the world of business knows it to be true. And doesn't it make sense?

If we face an important interview, we prepare ourselves to make the best possible impression. We look good. So, if we are about to meet an audience, we should polish our words as well as our shoes. We should sound good. Let's make that a first resolution.

BE YOUR OWN WRITER

Let's assume that you are prepared to do all your own background work—researching and writing the lines for the performance that you will eventually deliver. There are, of course, companies that offer script-writing services for a fee, and there is nothing to stop you from going to them if you wish. I have assumed, however, that you would not be reading this book if you were content to lean on a professional speechwriter. So, that makes two fields you need to conquer—the preparation of the speech, followed by its delivery. Where, though, do you begin? How do you go about getting your act together?

All speeches consist of a cleverly joined string of solutions to the cry "But I haven't an idea what to say." Ideas are the core and foundation of the whole thing, and collecting ideas is your starting point.

Keep a notebook. From this moment on, please use it to jot down anything you read or hear that just might be useful in a speech, no matter how remote the possibility. You might hear some wag in a bar say, "Did you know the war between Iran and Iraq was caused by a typing error?" and get a laugh for it. Just as soon as you can, note down "IRAN IRAQ TYPING ERROR". Maybe you'll never use it. But it might fit neatly into an address to your company about the purchase of new and expensive computers: "Better machinery can lead to fewer mistakes. And a single slip can cost more than an entire system. Good heavens, just look at the war between Iran and Iraq—all caused by a typing error."

Ideas Are Like Beansprouts—They Grow In The Dark

Originality wells up from mysterious and subconscious sources, and you must let the subterranean waters accumulate. Haven't you found that you can go to bed totally stumped for a solution to some problem, and wake up the next morning with an inspired answer? The same trick can come to your aid in preparing a speech.

Putting the matter to the back of your mind triggers that marvellous part of the brain where subconsciousness dwells. By concentrating your thoughts on the possible ways in which you could express your message you are also awakening your own instinctive ability to recognize the best method. And not only in sleep. Most professional writers know that the creative process can take place during all those times of the day when they are occupied with prosaic matters—shaving, taking a bath, mowing the lawn, walking the dog, even going to the bathroom.

Especially going to the bathroom, according to Noel Coward. He found that daily function was frequently accompanied by the arrival of a pleasing inspiration. Kingsley Amis, too, has written of his reliance upon casual meditation while carrying out some undemanding task or other, finding the rewards are his when he reaches the typewriter and begins to write. So much has already fallen into place. You are not faced with a dreaded sheet of blank paper but with a welcome page on which to arrange the ideas which have been floating to the surface of your mind and which now seem to demand expression.

So don't put off contemplating until the last minute. Muse as you munch, weigh while you wash, ponder when you perambulate; every pensive reflection will pay dividends when the time comes to collect your thoughts and say them out loud to an audience.

Your Script—
Putting The Right
Construction On It

It's time to lay out the shape of your speech and look at the basic elements in its construction. Lewis Carroll's White Rabbit was given some pretty clear advice:

"Where shall I begin, please your Majesty?" he asked.

"Begin at the beginning," the King said, gravely, "and go on till you come to the end: then stop."

IN THE BEGINNING

In the beginning is the hook. In show business terms a hook is any means of grabbing the crowd. Any good salesman uses various opening gambits to engage the attention of his customers. They range from the market trader's "Son, have I got a deal for you!" to the softer sell of "Don't rush me, these are like gold dust." One smooth talker opened his pitch to me with "I'm selling these computers below cost." I said, "How can you make money like that?" He said, "Repairing them." I laughed so much, I nearly bought one.

The start of every public presentation has a hook to it. Think of stage plays. In *The Man of Destiny* George Bernard Shaw shows us the 27-year-old Napoleon Bonaparte attacking all the courses of his meal simultaneously with his left hand while marking military positions on a map with his right. He calls for some red ink. The landlord of the Italian inn says, "Alas! Excellency, there is none." Napoleon answers, "Then kill something and bring me its blood." The grinning host replies that there is nothing but the general's own horse, the sentinel, the lady upstairs and his wife. Napoleon says, "Kill your wife." "Willingly, your Excellency," replies the man, but unhappily I am not strong enough. She would kill me." "That will do equally well," says Napoleon. During this wonderful exchange, we're wondering about the lady upstairs. We're hooked.

A great playwright such as Shaw knows that he has us at his disposal for the duration of Act One at least, so he has no need to grab us by the lapels from curtain-up, merely to put us in an interested state of mind. But remember that, as they planned their plays, shaped their plots and deployed their characters, they had a tough decision to make—where to start. No drama or novel ever has a single obvious starting point, there are hundreds to choose from. Who speaks first? How far into the story are we? How early was the outcome determined?

We have a similar choice to make with our speech. Should we go in loud and wake 'em up? Creep up quietly and lure them into listening? Use the carrot or the stick? The manner of your approach depends greatly upon your personal style and the image of yourself that you wish to project. But there are useful professional devices for taking charge of your audience and here are three—the Question, the Anniversary and the Surprise.

The Question Hook

Start by asking a question. It's a common enough oratorical ruse but often forgotten by speakers in the mildly nervous grip of composing that opening paragraph. The Question Hook can take many forms but we'll look at four dependable examples. First, the question that's immediately relevant to the people, the place and the time.

Question One: Special for Tonight

An expert on nutrition kicked off his after-dinner address by waving the menu in the air and asking, "How many calories do you think you've just consumed? How much protein? How much fat? How much carbohydrate? How much cholesterol or alcohol? Well, I am about to tell you and the answers will not only amaze you and amuse you, they will make you very proud of what your body can do."

This approach engaged everyone's attention because it was topical, personal and, although a little worrying, it contained a promise of good news. A similar strategy might suit you. Maybe there's something unique about the occasion: "What is it about this evening that makes it different from any other?" Or perhaps the audience has achieved a goal which you are about to announce: "Let me ask you a question about yourselves. Why have you, each and every one of you, a reason to feel proud today?"

That last application of the Question Hook introduces the second example.

Question Two: Let's Think About Ourselves

You open with a question that makes everyone present ask it of themselves. "If you had to describe yourself as a saint or a sinner, which would it be? No, seriously, do you think you're an angel or a devil? Put it this way: are you more good than bad or more bad than good? Now be careful. If any of you claim to be 100 per cent saintly, just remember this—a halo is only 10 inches from being a noose."

That speech went on to praise the charitable work of the audience while listing their daily sins with accuracy and good humor. The question had caused everyone in the room to make a small private assessment of themselves and made them readier to pay attention to what followed. This prodding of a person's ego may seem more like a conversational trick at a party, but it really does suit some speeches very well indeed.

7

I heard a distinguished attorney begin, "Think carefully before you answer this question, and I address it to each one of you individually. Have you ever broken the law?" It made a neat start to a list of small infringements that most of us commit regularly and unknowingly. Such questions help to involve the audience in subject matter that might not otherwise seem so attractive at first. If the body of your speech is a bit heavy, consider introducing it lightly with that sort of question.

Question Three: Off the Wall

Next there's the question that appears to have no relevance whatsoever. A social reformer began, "Why are there so many questions to which no-one knows the answers? Anybody?" He looked around so earnestly his audience couldn't help laughing at the intrinsic absurdity of what he was asking. Then he went on, "No, I don't know either. But I've got quite a few answers to questions not enough of us even bother to ask. And in offering you these answers I may step on a few toes today. Well, if I do I shall have to take comfort in the words of Winston Churchill: 'Any man who never steps on anyone else's toes is standing still!'"

By the way, it's worth noting that Churchill never said that. I've always found that attributing a good line to an admired wit increases its appreciation. Again, if I've got an old quip that's funny but familiar, I'll attribute it to a respected but dead comedian. Nobody argues about it, I'm not responsible for sounding corny and, as the audience laughs at the gag, I can see some of them nodding in apparent recollection of having heard it from the great late comic. I've even known a totally new pun that would normally pull a groan of agony from the crowd become magically transformed through wholly false attribution to Groucho Marx and score both hoots of mirth and nostalgic applause. "So what's to hurt?" as Harry S. Truman was always saying.

Question Four: Making Them Wonder

Lastly, a fourth version of the Question Hook is the presentation of a small mystery to the audience. In this example it was applied to a fairly serious and successful business gathering.

8

"There is a quality present in this room, a certain positive charge that I can sense very clearly. Every public speaker develops an instinctive feeling for unusual vibrations and this evening there is one powerful unifying force that I find quite unmistakable. What is it?" The pause need not be a long one before presenting the answer: "In a word—confidence. Behind us lies a great year for our industry, before us lies an even greater one. And you are the reason, you are the do-ers. While others have hesitated, you have acted. You've seen the size of the job and you've tackled it. You've learned the wisdom of what my old grandad used to say: "You can't plough a field by turning it over in your mind."

Having flattered his audience quite enough, the speaker is now free to emphasize the very weaknesses in the industry that he may have been setting out to identify in the first place. Because he has praised the audience, they will be more willing to receive his criticisms.

There are countless ways to employ the Question Hook. It can also come in handy as a way of closing: "And let me leave you with this question. . . ."

The Anniversary Hook

"Ladies and gentlemen, this is an historic day! This day, the 17th of December, will always be memorable for three great events. Orville Wright made the first successful flight in an airplane in 1903, Ludwig Van Beethoven had his first day on earth in 1770—and on this day in 1988 you attended tonight's banquet and heard the finest damned after-dinner speech of your entire lifetime! Now . . . who's going to make it?"

There's nothing like telling the people what a special day it is today. It has a feeling of topicality, even if the anniversaries named are ancient history, because you are telling them that "Today's the Day!" But where do you find such handy facts? There are quite a few reference books in the public libraries listing the chronology of great discoveries, births and deaths, publications, wars and battles, performances, treaties, exhibitions, laws, Nobel awards, inventions, statistics, sports events, films, plays, paint-

9

ings, economic and political events, even momentous speeches. Alas, few of them are very entertaining.

One such resource is *The Book of Days*, an encyclopedia of historical figures and events keyed to calendar days, ed., C. Edward Wall, 1987, Pierian Press. I wrote a Book of Days myself and I've been surprised at the number of public speakers who have told me of its usefulness to them. One wrote, "Whenever I'm stuck for an odd coincidence or a legitimate chuckle to get me off the ground I just check the date of the speech in the book and find some historical curiosity. One Leap Year I was desperate for a line to open a talk to a Musical Society on the last day of February—and there it was."

The item he found under 29 February ran: "Gioacchino Antonio Rossini was born today in 1792 in Pesaro, Italy. He wrote thirty-nine operas, including *The Barber of Seville* in 1816 and *William Tell* in 1829. When his 1826 opera *The Siege of Corinth* received a derogatory review, Rossini wrote to the critic: "Sir, I am sitting in the smallest room of my house. I have your review before me. In a moment it will be behind me."

In the hope that you may enjoy some similar serendipity, at the end of this book you will find a section headed "Special Occasions" with some newly gathered and amusing observations for the same. Anniversaries, births and deaths are always worth checking up on, and you can usually find a section in your local paper with such useful information. Not only can they provide natural openers, you'll find them equally useful for wrapping up a speech as well. For instance, September the 6th:

"In conclusion, ladies and gentlemen, this day marks another significant anniversary. On this day, September the 6th, back in 1901, U.S. President William McKinley was making a speech when some fellow shot him dead. Now I'm not much of a one for believing in signs and omens but there's no point in tempting fate so I think I'll sit down."

The Surprise Hook

"Before I start speaking, I have something to say," said one speaker and was bewildered by the laughter it provoked. He'd been delivering the same packaged twenty minutes for years but had just been asked to put in a preliminary announcement. What was so damned funny about that?

This speaker's unintentional absurdity points to another of the trade's opening stratagems—the unexpected statement or the Surprise Hook. By putting a startling remark ahead of your formal discourse, you catch the audience off-guard.

For example, it can be the expression of an attitude directly opposed to that commonly held, a small heresy that will create a shock-wave of attention. Imagine rising to address an enthusiastic Angling Society with these words:

"Fishing is the closest you can come to doing nothing at all without getting into politics."

After the briefest pause to let that unorthodox view register, you might add:

"Of course, I'm talking about *my* fishing, not yours. You are all true fishermen and women. I'm more of a birth-control device for worms. But that doesn't reduce my admiration for this Society, quite the opposite, etc. . . ."

Or picture the faces on an audience of Medical Practitioners as you begin:

"God heals, doctors take the fee."

And then continue:

"So said Benjamin Franklin and he's dead. I don't know who he blamed for that, his doctor or God. Of course, to many people a doctor is a sort of god, an all-powerful healer with mysterious powers. But, looking around me here, I am happy to see the very human side of professional medicine, etc. . . ."

An amusing make-believe drunk struggled to his feet and began, "How long have I been on?"

At a lunchtime function followed by a lengthy speech by a government official, the author Ian Fleming merely looked at his wristwatch and began, "Good evening." In similar circumstances at an evening function he might have created the same amusing effect by saying, "Good morning."

Whatever angle the Surprise Hook takes—the controversial statement quickly reversed into a tribute, the wry comment on the present situation ahead of your more sedate opening, the plainly off-beat or the out-of-character—this particular way into your material is the trickiest I know and needs careful and con-

11

fident use. I would never recommend it to a novice speaker. But when the occasion is right and the speaker's first words contain a little shock, the effect can be surprisingly good.

Another Opening, Another Show

Now let's consider some classic opening gambits. Remember this gem from David Niven? "Tonight I feel like Zsa Zsa Gabor's fifth husband. I know what to do but how do I make it interesting?"

Another speaker took that line and twisted it ingeniously: "This is like making love to Joan Collins. You know it's been done before many, many times. And much, much better."

Here's another way of using the same joke: "Thank you, ladies and gentlemen. I feel like the young Arab sheik who inherited his father's harem. I know what to do but where the hell do I begin?"

Try this different twist: "Thank you. As Henry VIII said to each of his wives in turn, "I shall not keep you long."

The elements are clear enough. The speaker is referring to his current situation, the fact that he is about to address us. Compare this relationship between speaker and audience to that between a man and a woman. It's a dilemma for the man. In what circumstances does a man face such a dilemma? On his wedding night. Greater still is the dilemma and funnier if his bride has been married before—more than once. Thus the Zsa Zsa joke. Suppose she is famous for having lovers as well as husbands. Thus the Joan Collins joke. Who else faces a sexual challenge? An Arab sheik in his seraglio. Should we make him impotent? No, because by implication this suggests the speaker is incapable of performing. Thus the young sheik joke. How can you use this same sexual comparison to assure the audience that you're not going to talk lengthily? What man dealt briefly with his women? Casanova? Yes, but like Don Juan he is remembered for passion and we don't want the audience to get overexcited; it's not that kind of a get-together. Bluebeard? Yes, but that analogy implies murdering the people. Henry VIII is the perfect fellow. The variations are infinite.

12

IN THE MIDDLE

"Expounding your theme"—"Warming to your subject"—"Preaching your message"—the ways in which the central part of a speech can be described are generally as vague as those hackneyed phrases because only you, the speaker, know the exact nature of the material you have to deliver.

The body of any specific address, whether it's for a Stag Party, a Fund Raiser, Sales Conference, Twenty-first Birthday, Regimental Banquet, Temperance Lecture, Product Launch, Engagement Party, Garden Fete, Assembly Hall Welcome, Rotary Lunch, Ladies' Night, Exhibition Opening, Christening or Bar Mitzvah, must express in essence what *you* know and feel and trust is right for the occasion. The information you have to impart has to be yours, not mine. And yet the manner in which you convey it can be analyzed and perfected. Together we can make sure you are never one of those speakers who stumble along, spreading their own banana peels in front of them.

First and always, and I make no apology for repeating myself because an essential truth deserves constant reiteration, please research and prepare your topics. Know more about them than you need to know. The more information you have in reserve, the more selective you can be about what you choose to say.

Then find suitable sub-headings, deal with them in order and lighten them with just enough well-chosen quotations, asides, anecdotes and personal observations to amuse, inform and satisfy the expectations of your listeners. Just enough, not overkill.

You should never lose sight of two objectives:
1. *What you intend to accomplish* and
2. *What the audience requires.*

In other words, attain a balance between what you want to say and what they want to hear.

Keep the Audience in the Story

Whenever you depart from the main thrust to make ancillary points, demonstrate to your audience how each of your secondary subjects is relevant to them. Keep their particular group attitude in mind and find ways to personalize even the most remote issue so that they can see a connection between themselves and it. If people can see how what you're telling them applies to their own lives, they remain interested.

Use Generosity, Generously

If your speech is a social one, return to its human strengths often. Never overlook the four elements of a social speech which are almost impossible to overdo:

Welcome, Congratulate, Salute and Thank.

Give these courtesies generously to all who will expect and warm to such references. If you pull someone's leg, sugar the joke with praise. As one speaker wrote, "Praise is a kind of spiritual vitamin." And Lord Chesterfield said, "I never knew any man deserve praise who did not desire it."

It's a funny thing, but even effusive praise need not sound sycophantic in a speech. The same flattery that could appear too florid or subservient when spoken in private seems quite acceptable in a public tribute. Often, the teasing jibe and the sincere acknowledgement fit well together:

"And what can I say about our dear friend Wally Walters that hasn't already been said in open court? Tonight it's good to see Wally relaxing and letting his hair down for a change. And it is a change to see Wally letting something down because one thing's certain, Wally. You've never let down a customer or a friend."

Know Your History

In a social speech, after ensuring that no speaker ahead of you will have done so, you can plan to include the story of the Society's origins and dedicated aims. If you do, be sure to check up on every detail to be certain of accuracy. I've known a somnolent mob snap to critical attention when a guest speaker made one mistake about the history of their organization.

Using Humor Without Depending on Laughs

When you enliven serious points with appropriate stories, choose them with ingenuity and reconsider them with care. Does the humorous story arise naturally from the serious words that precede it? Does its punchline act as a punctuation at the end of a paragraph so that you can embark smoothly on the next new topic? Or do you want to use the punchline as continuity for the serious point to follow it? You'll find a hundred such examples in the chapter "In and Out of Humorous Classics".

I recommend that you always try to choose stories that have a telling point. In that way, if the tale fails to win a laugh, you can go right on talking as if you never meant it to. Then it appears that your only reason for telling the story was its message. When you weave such anecdotes into your speech to form a seamless flow, you take out what professional comedians call "insurance". In short, if they don't laugh, they won't know they haven't.

The Audience: How Big, How Small?

In preparing the major part of what you want to say, take into consideration the size of the audience. I once had to present a plan for a promotional advertising campaign to the clients and their advertising agency. Expecting a boardroom and anything up to a dozen faces, I wrote a very brief pitch with photographs and illustrations that could be passed from hand to hand during a question-and-answer session in which most of my major selling points would be developed. When I arrived I found a conference hall with three hundred people, mostly composed of the sales force for the product. I had no slides to display, no photo blow-ups, no big speech setting out all the reasons behind my plan of campaign and enumerating its virtues. It took all my performing skills to save the situation. They weren't enough to save the campaign.

It could have been just as bad if I had prepared an address for three hundred and found myself in an office with three. Stuck with ten pages of carefully paced explanation leading to a summing up, I'd have been drawn into a discussion before page two. As one effective speaker used to say, "The size of my performance is related to the number of tickets sold."

Short Speeches Are Not Always the Best—But the Best Speeches Always Seem Short

Like a good piece of music, your speech has a natural duration. Like music, it may have a single theme or more than one, harmoniously related to each other. Like music—and like this paragraph—it can be repetitive for effect. But if you'll forgive one more analogy, it's like a bad tooth—the more slowly it is drawn out, the more it hurts.

One speaker put it well: "There's a great power in words, if you don't hitch too many of them together."

The most obvious limitation upon the length of your speech is the time available for it. Establish this at the outset. How long do they want you to speak? How long do you want to talk to them? Plan the content of your speech accordingly, timing it if you can. If you have a tendency to expand on favorite topics or ramble a little for effect, keep an easily visible watch where the audience cannot see you checking it too openly, and try to obey its discipline. Referring to your wristwatch can be an unfortunate gesture, making you appear more concerned with time than with your message and with the company you're keeping. It's also a silent reminder to your audience of how long you've been talking. Unless you have an amusing pleasantry to cover such a move, it's one I'd avoid.

16

Knowing When To Get Off

A warm laugh, a spontaneous round of applause or perhaps just a concerted murmur of general agreement—these can often be a signal to the speaker to quit while he's ahead. Never feel you have to cover every point you've prepared in advance. No-one but you knows what you have planned to say, and if the mood in the room strikes you as the ideal one in which to close, simply cut and go into your finish. It's a matter of not just listening to yourself but listening to your audience as well. Maybe the message they're sending you is "Carry on, we could listen to you all night"... but maybe it's not.

You may have been an onlooker when a performer has reached just such a moment and you may have sighed inwardly when the rapport that should have existed between him and his audience failed to operate his stop-light. I have also been in many a mixed gathering which had more patience with a good song well sung than with a full recital. So keep your antenna tuned to the audience's transmitter and be prepared to fold your tent at any time.

IN THE END

Some speakers feel uneasy about ending their speeches with humour. They reckon that if they are putting over a serious message it will be weakened by a lightweight conclusion. Margaret Thatcher's speechwriter would concur. He makes judicious use of wit in the early segments but hardens to closing passages of short sharp fact, rhythmic repetition and inspirational uplift.

The American poet Robert Frost advised that poems should begin in delight but end in wisdom. However, wit and wisdom are often contained in the same sentence, and offering both to your audience before regaining your seat would seem to be a worthwhile endeavor. Speaking from experience, I've found that a shrewdly chosen tale which combines truth with fun is a far more popular finale than either a glum proverb, an exhortation to work harder or a declaration of some philosophical principle. Apart from which, there are other advantages besides the goodwill that's generated by telling a good closing story. For one thing, a knockout punch will often make an audience forget a poorly conducted fight and, likewise, many an indifferently received oration has been saved by a verbal k.o. in the closing seconds.

Finding the Ideal Ending

In a speech to celebrate the acquisition of an island by a Socialist millionaire, I sought an anecdote to illustrate as neatly as possible his famous balance of left-wing politics, capitalism and outspoken honesty about himself. Here's how I wrapped up my address:

"I've never known anyone as frankly, fearlessly and funnily truthful about himself as Len. There is simply no better example of this blatant self-exposure of his true nature than this—and I can't follow it so I'll close with it.

"Len had just paid the asking price for his island in the sun where never again will he need to put on his hated dinner suit—that's right, it's a sort of tux haven—yes, he had no sooner proclaimed himself lord of his domain, uncorked a Jeroboam of Dom Perignon and poured me a mugful when I asked him to explain his political philosophy.

"What I actually asked Len was, 'What do you consider the object of Government?' Unhesitatingly and very earnestly Len said, 'The greatest good for the greatest number.' 'And what,' I asked, 'do you consider to be the greatest number?' And Len said, 'Number one."

As the long laugh ebbed I raised my glass and said, "Ladies and gentlemen, the toast is . . . Number One!" I had rounded off my speech with the ring of witty truth and no-one seemed to recall a very similar tale being told about the scholar and philosopher David Hume two hundred years earlier. Searching through my files of good historical anecdotes, I'd found an almost perfect fit and made minor adjustments. You can do the same. Just try to look at all your source material with a fresh eye to see if it will match your subject. Don't feel bound by factual accuracy. If you take an ideal line by Voltaire and put it in the mouth of the Chief Accountant, it's unlikely that anyone but a student of 18th-century literature is going to care. A speech is an entertainment containing whatever information you wish to convey. After all, it's not going to be reviewed by any literary critics. We're in practical territory here and we use whatever material answers our needs.

Use Anything That Works For You

One well-known speaker told me he needed to end his speech on an apt line about a Managing Director who never stopped urging his sales force to strive harder for bigger rewards and whose wife was widely reputed to be a big spender. What he said was, "I cannot do better than end with the words of our Managing Director. Jack once said, and I quote, 'There's only one thing a man can do if he's married to a wife who enjoys spending money, and that is—learn to enjoy earning it!"

As the gathering dispersed, a visitor made his way to the top table and buttonholed the speaker. "Say, that last line you told us you heard from Jack . . . it's a direct quote from Ed Howe." "Good Lord!" said the speaker, "So Jack's a plagiarist."

The Top-and-Tail Effect

If no ideal anecdote or quotation offers itself to you, there's a professional device known as "bracketing". The two brackets consist of a set-up at the top of your script and a pay-off at the end. Many humorous lyrics and monologues use this trick, establishing a phrase at the outset and then leading to the same phrase amusingly repeated to round off the last line. The great popular lyricist Ira Gershwin loved brackets. In his song "But Not For Me", for example:

"They're writing songs of love,
But not for me,
A lucky star's above,
But not for me ..."

How does he collect on his title line? Right at the end, of course:

"When ev'ry happy plot
Ends with the marriage knot,
And there's no knot for me."

Brackets can serve you well in a speech. The words you will end with are planted clearly at the start, like this:

"I asked the Chairman what he thought was my mission here today and his advice was typically forthright: 'Stand up, speak up and sit down.' I asked him to elucidate. He said, 'Certainly. Stand up so our members can see you, speak up so our members can hear you, and then sit down so our members can enjoy themselves."

That's your first bracket, set up briefly first of all, then in more expanded form to make it even more memorable. It's amusing enough on its own. It's even possible to use its construction in triplicate by employing it in the fabric of your speech, employing secondary meanings for each pair of words. "Stand up" can mean standing up for your beliefs, "Speak up" can be interpreted as speaking up for the weak or the sick, "Sit down" to signify the need to go to the negotiating table and confer. Those are optional extras, of course, and whether you explore them or not, your opening paragraph has established the nature of your closing paragraph, as follows:

"Let's see, I think that's everything. My mission here today was clearly explained to me, if you recall. (*Consult a piece of paper*

20

as though reading your instructions.) 'Stand up so our members can see you'—I've done that. 'Speak up so our members can hear you'—I trust I've done that. 'Sit down so our members can enjoy themselves.' (_Tearing the paper neatly in two_) "Mission accomplished!"

Notice too how the repetition of the word "mission" helps the open-and-closed nature of the brackets, giving extra symmetry.

Always make the end of your speech a definite completion, not a sudden dismissal or a dying fizzle. It's easier in a formal or business speech when you can summarize, repeat all your main headings, maybe demand action based upon your words, hammer home a slogan or finish on a visual display. But even in a social speech there are useful conventions. You can wish the Society and its members good fortune in the future, repeat your thanks, quote their motto, raise another toast, or even recite a poem. Believe me, you could do a lot worse than verse. Anything that rhymes wraps up an act. Listen, if it was good enough for Shakespeare . . .

If you want to finish on a neat, amusing line, I offer a handful of suggestions below. But safety comes first, and if it's safety you want I recommend one of these three endings. For total security, use all three.

Sincerity

When you mean it deeply, return to it, say it again from the heart.

Salesmanship

If you've got an angle, serious or light-hearted, sock it to them.

Wit and Wisdom

If you got the right anecdote to close, nothing can follow it.

"And In Conclusion, Ladies and Gentlemen . . ."

What welcome words those can be. Someone once described them as "a wake-up call for audiences." If you fancy sitting down to a chuckle, here are some suitable "let-me-leave-you-with-this-thought" sort of lines:

"Remember, there are Seven Deadly Sins, enough for one for each day, so . . . have a nice week!"

"And please drive home carefully. We'd all much rather talk *to* you than *about* you."

"And please—don't learn the traffic regulations by accident. Try to drive so that your license expires before you do."

"And finally, friends, if you want instant relief from that dull, incessant headache . . . good night!"

"In these stressful times, take care of your heart. With all these transplants, some day *I* might get it."

"Before I sit down I'd like to thank you for being a wonderful audience . . . and you can feel proud because I'm very hard to please."

"A final thought. Always keep your words nice and sweet—because you never know when you're going to have to eat them."

Etiquette and All That

If the occasion is formal, correct titles and forms of address should be equally formal. First on your roster must be the person in the chair, either "Mr. Chairman" or "Madam Chairman", "Mr. President" or "Madam President". If sexual equality is your topic, you may prefer to begin, "Honored Chairperson . . ."

Addressing Public Officials

The President of the United States is addressed as "Mr. President", as is the Vice President and the Chief Justice of the Supreme Court. The First Lady is the only woman official not to be addressed by her given name. Members of the Cabinet, the Speaker of the House, the Attorney General, Senators, Representatives, Ambassadors, Governors, State Senators, State Representatives, Mayors, Judges, and the heads of agencies are addressed as "The Honorable". All others are addressed as "Mr." and "Madam".

Kings Don't Come First

Second on the formal list comes royalty. The way to address a ruling sovereign is "Your Majesty", and the correct way to address a member of the Royal Family is "Your Royal Highness". After the person in the chair and any Royalty that's wandered in looking for a lost corgi, you should extend acknowledgment to whichever other individuals you consider worthy of the honour: "Mr. Chairman, Your Royal Highness, My Lord Bishop, Madam Mayor, Mr. Bob Monkhouse, My Lords, Ladies, and Gentlemen. . . ."

What's Bob Monkhouse doing in there? Well, I'm using my name as though I were the person to whose speech you are replying. That's where such a name goes in the list—after the top brass and before "My Lords, Ladies and Gentlemen".

And the Rest of the Field

Who else might be there? A Duke or a Marquis? Just add the magic words "My Lord" or "My Lady" and you have the correct form of address, e.g. "My Lord Duke", "My Lady Marchioness", etc. Vice- Presidents get a Mr. or Madam in front of their titles. Prime Ministers are addressed as just that. They're used to being called a lot worse.

If the Church is represented, the Archbishop is "Your Grace", the Dean is "Very Reverend Sir", and the Archdeacon is "Venerable Sir". That's all I know about addressing the clergy because I've never been much of a churchgoer, just baptisms, weddings and funerals. What our local priest calls a "three sprinkle job".

An Ambassador is "Your Excellency" and, as in all instances above, is simply referred to as "Sir" or "Madam" thereafter. Having a Knighthood doesn't make you a Lord, of course, so you lump any present under that final "Ladies and Gentlemen", unless you're mentioning a particular name such as "Sir Bob Geldof". But he doesn't attend many formal functions because he finds them depressing. And they do say that when Sir Bob gets very depressed he just hangs about the house, clean-shaven.

Oh Lord, You Made the Night Too Long

You only have to look at the menu of a formal dinner party to see the pattern of the evening ahead of you. Discounting the courses of food, prepared without regard to your diet and wines often chosen without regard to your palate, just look at those speeches. There's:

The Loyal Toast

Someone, a toastmaster if there's one booked, will bang on the table and propose the toast to the organization, followed by the simultaneous ignition of lighters, matches and cigarettes.

The Toast to the Society

Now someone rattles on, briefly if fate is kind, about the history and purpose and recent concerns of the circle. And just when you thought that was it, you get:

The Response

The President or the Chairman says thank you and sits down. That, at least, is an ideal Response. In the More Frequently Encountered Response, he grabs his chance to puff up his own achievements during the past year and, unless prevented, kill off a few more smiles by listing those members who have kicked the bucket. Are you ready for your introduction? I hope so because here is:

The Toast to the Ladies and Guests

One of your hosts names the principal guests, saving you for last so that he can describe your qualifications for claiming the attention of all present. Whereupon you rise to deliver:

25

The Response

This is the principal speech of the whole enchilada, including or concluding with your thanks to the hosts on behalf of yourself and all the other guests. The Chairman may rise finally to thank you, but that's a sort of optional extra. And so to bed.

ALL RULES HAVE THEIR EXCEPTIONS—EXCEPT THIS

Of the many hard and fast rules for success in public speaking, nearly all are hard and none are fast. There is one, however, that holds faster than all the others. This is:

Always Have Someone Introduce You

Never introduce yourself. Even if you are very, very famous and everyone knows you're coming and the organizers assure you there's no need to announce your name, always insist on an introduction. And don't leave the wording of the announcement to chance—write a short, explicit, honest intro and have it with you. Ask the person introducing you if he is happy with his own words or would he prefer to use yours. Make it clear that this is just you being helpful, not an ego trip, so will he please resist trying to score a cheap laugh by telling the audience that you provided your own intro. I'm sure you can put this politely but firmly. Only if you feel confident that the person announcing you can do it well should you leave it to him. (I'd give him your prepared intro anyway; there may be a vital fact about you he doesn't know.) If the room is busy or noisy, ask him to quiet the crowd and get them settled before he goes into your introduction. Be resolute on this point: Like a painting needs a frame. Like a singer needs an accompaniment, like Royalty needs a fanfare—you need an introduction.

To Yourself Be True

The central dilemma facing many amateur speakers may be put thus: if a comedian says funny things, and a comic says things funny, what should an ordinary speaker do?

Well, unless the speaker is a gifted comedian or comic, he can take a much simpler but equally effective course to win his laughs—play it straight. Over many years I have observed a speaker who, constantly in demand for his wonderfully funny speeches, never attempted to act funnily. He maintained a sober demeanor, smiling rarely and only when the moment seemed right. He surveyed the room with a friendly gaze but remained deadpan as he delivered his most hilarious lines. He never mugged or assumed a ridiculous accent or mimicked a character in his narrative or essayed zany gestures. This great humorous speaker left broad comedy performance to the professional clowns. He knew that his best way of telling a joke was seriously. You too can use this approach to rewarding effect.

THE DEADPAN DELIVERY OF DAVID FROST

Adopt the role of a raconteur. This way, you can score your best laughs by doing less, not more. David Frost is one brilliant speaker who knows that he is least amusing when clowning and most amusing when appearing to be either earnest or offhand. He therefore delivers his wittiest sentences more like a commentator than a comic and is all the funnier for it.

I sat beside him at a luncheon for British television star, Terry Wogan, and saw how carefully David listened to the earlier speakers, jotting down a note of anything they said which he felt could be usefully referred to in his own speeches. After his introduction from the toastmaster, he stood with a single page held casually in his hand and took a moment to look around him as though weighing up the audience and finding them satisfactory. "Hello, good evening, and Wogan!" That was his first laugh.

Next came an early chance to cash in on the rapt attention he had given to previous speakers. One of them had referred, in passing, to Terry's TV commercials. David had immediately asked my wife which commercial Terry was doing. She said it was for a margerine. David had scribbled, "Butter/marge." Now he continued, "It's a great privilege to be here today and to speak about a man who, as we all know, can really tell margarine from butter. . . ." David paused to allow a mild laugh to pass, then went on, "Margarine *pays* better."

Then he made a gesture with the notes as if they were inadequate for his purpose. "What do you say about Terry Wogan?" he went on. "A man who, in some circles, is spoken of as a god. 'God, is he on again?' they say." David shook his head as though in dumb admiration. "Just out of hospital, of course, after a painful operation, having three Blarney Stones removed; sometimes described as a sort of Irish Eamonn Andrews . . ." By not pausing for a laugh on the mild Blarney Stone line, David could now take a beat to collect a laugh made larger by that strategy.

Still unsmiling to indicate the seriousness of his tribute, he repeated the name. "Terry Wogan! A man who spends half his time turning down marriage proposals from lady admirers . . . and the rest of his time autographing their bus passes." Allowing a long laugh to develop and fade, David looked at his notes just long enough to see the words "Books/income." An earlier speaker had made reference to Terry's best-selling books. "I'm delighted that tribute has been paid already to his literary works," he continued. "My favorite is the one he wrote as he became more and more wealthy—*I Upped My Income—Up Yours*." This is not a new joke but how cleverly David used it, making the arrogance of the book title appear to come from Terry, not from him.

Having given the audience enough special material about the guest of honor, David could now afford to change the subject and produced the well-tested substance of previous successful speeches. Still he maintained a reporter's air of communication, pacing the phrases steadily and stressing key words with that famous Frost emphasis, and never allowing more than the merest trace of a smile to break the mood. As he continued on the theme of famous bloopers, he contrived to keep the guest of honor in the frame: "But Terry's not on this list because he's so damned articulate"—and from there he went on with more hilarious goofs by assorted celebrities and won more big laughs from the audience.

Suddenly David put his notes down on the table. It was a deliberate, theatrical tactic. It seemed to say, "We've all had a good laugh, now I'm no longer fooling." His tone softened and his mock sincerity was replaced by the genuine article. He said, "It's not that long ago that I first met Terry. I was on his program and I strolled in to say hello to Terry, we'd never met before, this was back in April—and about three weeks later I wanted to give Terry a book and I was inscribing it. And I just wrote inside the front, 'To Terry—an old friend in three weeks flat.' And that's the way we all respond to him, a man who inspires immediate and sincere friendship from everyone. And so Terry Wogan, the man who put the corn in leprechaun, we salute you." And David sat down to warm and well deserved applause.

BE YOURSELF MADE LARGE

As you will have realized, I regard David Frost as an exemplary speaker. But my reason for quoting that speech of David's at such length is not so much to demonstrate its excellent construction and content as to show how little the speaker had to do in its performance. If you had videotaped that speech and played it back with the sound turned off, you would be surprised at the economy of motion, the absence of sly grins and assumed outrage. Like David Frost, you don't need any elaborate apparatus to put over a sharply funny address. You can just be yourself made large.

A good politician knows his subject, his audience, his comedy and drama, and the fastest way out. A good speaker knows all of these together with a serenity denied to those who practice politics.

I would add to a good speakers's required knowledge the awareness of his own energy. Comedy is greatly to do with energy, both energy expended and energy reserved. The explosive clown is an obvious instance of energy expended. But the quiet magnetic attraction of an assertive personality, of latent power, of sheer presence—that's your ace in the hole. Your confidence in your command of the situation is a silent force, working invisibly to your advantage. You may imagine yourself as a Porsche holding back to a perfect cruising speed, knowing you can burst forward into a blur of motion if you feel like it. That's why it pays to play it straight. Cool as an announcer. Giving the Frost report.

THAT VOICE—CAN IT BE YOU?

Most of us are astonished the first time we hear our own voice. The resonant tones we've heard in our heads seem thin and alien issuing from a tape recorder. And that can make some prospective speakers feel apprehensive. Self-consciousness about the quality of your voice might tend to inhibit you. So let's deal with that worry. Let's think about some of our top personalities and most effective communicators. Ronald Reagan is known for his fuzzy thinking and his artful stammer. President Bush takes a lot of kidding for his vague verbiage. Dustin Hoffman is one of our finest actors but his voice is thin and nasal. So is Woody Allen's. Henry Kissinger would win no elocution contest with his perenially thick Teutonic accent. And Dr. Ruth is another prime candidate for a course in speaking standard, American English.

Who could categorize the amazing vocal gyrations of Howard Cosell? Barbara Walters has taken a lot of kidding in her day for her slightly impedimented 'r's,' and Malcolm Muggeridge doesn't speak so much as ooze. There is nothing of the mighty orator about any of them. They cannot declaim like Olivier or purr like Gielgud. When first encountered, they may not have impressed you as particularly expert speakers. But that initial impression can fool you. Very soon after you first adjusted your ears to these unusual voices, I'm sure you began to absorb what they had to say.

What you say is so much more important than how you say it. Great communicators and persuasive actors can make a lot out of a little, it's true, but a speaker without a powerful or melodious voice can register just as convincingly as soon as the audience tunes into the sense and caring behind his words.

All the famous and successful folk listed above stopped worrying about their voices long ago, if they ever did. They are each concerned with putting across their ideas. They speak to us with conviction, sincerity, urgency—and sometimes fun. If you offer your common sense and your humor and your heart to any audience, they cannot resist. People may smile at your voice when they first hear you, but it will not obscure your message in the end.

Rehearse—
And Make It Better

Friends who tell you not to worry should worry you. When they say, "No need to rehearse, it'll be okay on the night," that's a red light flashing. You won't be okay on the night if you're unprepared and under-rehearsed. It's so easy and so much more enjoyable, for you as well as your audience, when you know just exactly what you're doing. *And all that takes is time.*

Let's assume you've organized your speech and worked out most of the lines. You've set out your objectives, developed the principal themes, and built in the touches of humor that are right for you and right for the crowd. During this process of speech construction your grasp of its outline and essentials has strengthened and this has increased your confidence. It's almost as clear in your head as it is on paper. Now you're all set to deliver. It's time to identify possible traps.

Now what should we avoid? Well, you don't want to be the Rev. Billy Graham for a start, so let's not practice this speech with the booming voice of an orator. Neither do you want to turn into Chevy Chase overnight, so we won't parade the tricks of a full-time comedian. You're not giving a display of elocution, so there is no need to behave like a dialogue coach giving a lesson. In short, extremes are what we should avoid. And rehearsal helps us to iron them out.

Just as in the rehearsal of a play, when the director refines and adjusts the performance of each player, you should listen to yourself speaking your part. Be kind but be critical. Are you sounding so over-emphatic as to appear unpleasantly aggressive? Or is your delivery so bland and calm that it could seem indifferent?

You can choose from several rehearsal methods. Some speakers like to be isolated and unheard in a distant room, with or without a mirror. Others perform their speeches again and again to a sympathetic spouse or chum, either encouraging suggestions from them or requiring nothing more than a repeated hearing to ease away inhibitions.

Getting the Whole Thing Taped

A cassette recorder can be a blessing. I know an expert speaker who is an insurance broker. He tapes all his speeches, his sales pitches and his statistical backup—everything he needs to have on the tip of his tongue. Then he climbs into his Mercedes 500 SL and pops his cassette into the tape deck. All the way to each appointment he listens to himself talk, hears his weaknesses, learns his strengths, spots his omissions, and discovers new and better ways to express himself. On the passenger seat beside him is the little recorder. Whenever he gets a better idea, he puts the car player on pause and speaks his new idea into the recorder. Fussy? I can only tell you it gets great results. And, so far, no road accidents.

If you're taking part in a corporate presentation you may be able to arrange to have your final rehearsals put on videotape. Have you ever seen yourself on a TV screen? Now that's a real revelation. Every dull note, pointless gesture, stiff expression, unnecessary line and ugly stance is mercilessly recorded by the camera. It may make you wince and shudder but you'll learn a lot from it. The playback will tell you about your performance in a cruel way what a good stage director would tell you tactfully.

During auditions we videotape every act. When a comedian qualifies for a call-back, we tape him again. If he's booked for the show, we show him the tape. Shock, embarrassment, humiliation, disgust—I've seen all those reactions to the playback. I've also seen moments of appreciation for a nicely judged pause or a perfectly exercised grimace. Mostly, after that, I've seen instant improvement.

Rehearsing Your Other Speakers

It's worth sharing the rules of preparation and practice with any others on the bill with you. If you're in a position to insist, do so. And if you can record each run-through either on sound or video, so much the better. Let them see their first attempt and then, after discussions and alterations, show them how much better they appear a second or even a third time. Everything improves—timing, manner, content, projection, even an enhanced feeling of importance.

All this repetition and trial by recording also affords you the luxury of cutting out the deadwood. Now it just may be that when you weed out a weak passage in a speech, there is an obvious need to replace it. For example, there's the occasional anecdote that suddenly doesn't seem to fit or which the speaker no longer feels so sure about. The answer: always keep a few good stories and extra lines in your locker to fill in those gaps when and if required. It happens all the time in the theatre and TV studios—last-minute substitutions are made, unclear points are underpinned with a memorable new observation, and often such urgent changes prove to be more successful than the surrounding material.

THE PRACTICE OF PRACTICING

All this rehearsal business may seem irksome but, as I've found to my benefit, when I work hard for the me who's got to make the speech, I'm my own best friend. Enough practice helps you to:

1. Get Used to the Words

By saying them out loud, your mind and your mouth become accustomed to the phrases. You smooth out any awkward juxtaposition of words. You suddenly think of a way of saying a stuffy sentence in a more straightforward and colloquial style. And you take care that what might have been a hastily prepared text contains no nasty surprises for you when you have to deliver it.

2. Keep Your Eye on the Ball

Running over your main message, the lesser points, the supporting humor, etc., helps to put the whole speech in focus. It becomes so much a part of you that you can achieve the finest possible balance between your written notes and your memorized lines. And you will never lose sight of the ball.

3. Rid Yourself of First-Night Fright

Why do some actors freeze or fumble on the opening night, the very same actors who will bring off the same play a few evenings later with total aplomb? It's fear of unfamiliarity. They're also putting their jobs on the line but that's unlikely to be the outcome of a poorly delivered speech at any function, so let's set aside the professional anxiety.

No, first-night fright is mainly caused by the uncertainty of doing the unfamiliar. The more familiarity with the assignment, the less fear. Therefore, the more rehearsal, the more certainty of success and the greater peace of mind. The actors I've seen standing in the wings, waiting to make their entrance on a first night, may be tense and apprehensive for a hundred reasons. But if they have rehearsed thoroughly enough, they are never frightened. Most of the good ones can't wait to get out there. I'd like you to feel the same. (If you need more on this, see the chapter "Fears and Fallacies".)

Whatever form of rehearsal you favor, in private or with a companion, try to reproduce in your mind the circumstances of your finished performance. Speak as you will speak then, perhaps not with as much volume but as clearly and as well paced. Stand as you will stand then, not seated or reclining. Until you practice thinking and speaking aloud on your feet, you haven't rehearsed what will actually happen.

SHOULD YOU TAKE A GOOD LOOK AT YOURSELF?

Personally, I've never much liked using a mirror for rehearsal. It's useful for a dance routine, a comedy mime or a visual bit with a prop of some kind. But for a monologue I find it a bit like talking to myself instead of my imagined audience. You tend to become too concerned with your clothing and how cute you look. On the other hand, I know several fine performers who use a full-length mirror very cleverly, aware of the dangers of vanity overwhelming their better instincts and employing the reflection solely for information which will add to the final presentation.

That said, I still think you should beware of too much communing with the looking-glass. It can produce a self-centered state of mind which inhibits communication. But, as I've said elsewhere, try to check your appearance as near to showtime as possible. Some things can always be improved, like that lipstick kiss on your jowl or an unzipped fly.

WHAT SORT OF PERSON CAN HELP YOU REHEARSE?

Because performing experimentally doesn't embarrass me, I can try out new material on my wife or a co-writer immediately and expect to gain something from their reaction. But assuming you're not a hardened old campaigner like me, I think you should approach this carefully. It's very useful to find someone whose opinion you respect as a sounding board but not necessarily in the early stages of your practice. At that beginning period you are only just coming to grips with the elements of your speech and words of criticism can be unhelpful and discouraging, damaging the development of what could become your later strengths. I suggest you get the speech under your belt a bit before you try it out on anyone. After that, the input of trusted and caring listeners can be tremendously valuable. But watch out—they may want you to do the same for them some day. So don't choose bores.

HOW MUCH REHEARSAL IS ENOUGH?

If you were starring in a Broadway musical you might have to rehearse for a dozen weeks before your opening. But rehearsals don't stop there. Top directors keep a constant watch on their shows and as soon as they spot a performance slackening or a scene beginning to change shape, they call in the cast for renewed rehearsals, again and again. There's no such thing as too much rehearsal while further improvement is possible.

No-one can tell you how often you should practice your speech but the surest policy is: do it until you can't do it any better without the audience itself. If you have the chance of a run-through in the actual location for your speech, grab it. Likewise, if you can present your speech beforehand to a small group of colleagues or friends who understand what you are trying to achieve, grab that too. A dry run enables you to anticipate the reactions of your later, larger audience, and associates can often come up with the most unexpectedly helpful ideas. They'll pick on a word you're not saying clearly enough, ask you to expand on a point that's insufficiently clear, even add to your confidence with their keen attention and reassurance. If they happen to be in your employ, they might even give you three cheers as well.

Lastly, remember the old test used to judge advertising ideas—is the idea working for you, or do you have to work for it? You'll find that repeated practice is often the best way to recognize those parts of your speech which work for you and those which are hard to put across or simply not worth including. Keep in mind the following:

"A good speech is like a good boot—it won't wear out from polishing."

Fears And Fallacies

Asked to tell the secret of his comedy, a famous comedian answered, "Fear!"

Fear is nothing to be frightened of. It's natural and normal and it can be used as a positive force.

You would have to be insensitive, inhuman or very drunk if the prospect of public failure did not bother you at all. But it has been an essential part of my Monkhouse Method to analyze that worry and employ it as my ally. You can do the same.

FEAR IS YOUR FRIEND

First of all, consider what danger does to the human system. When you are frightened the sympathetic nerves are excited and adrenalin is poured into the blood from your adrenal glands, two little triangles just above your kidneys. This chemical reaction is vital in energizing your body to deal with the emergency. The mom who sees her child run into the road or the athlete gearing up for a race both have this sudden surge of adrenalin. It triggers those symptoms we know all too well—the pounding heart, rapid pulse, sweaty palms—but it is also mobilizing sugar from the liver to provide instant energy.

Your reflexes are sharpened and your nervous system with its countless switches, junctions and evaluation centers will use its incomparable skill to channel constant streams of nerve impulses towards the proper decision and action. So trust your stage fright. It's working for you, it's on your side. All you have to do is learn to use these desirable effects, to take and keep control of the vitality they bring you.

I once stood beside the urbane Dean Martin in the wings of the London Palladium. He calmly awaited the music for his entrance with no outward signs of tension. A stagehand looked at him curiously and asked, "Not nervous, Mr Martin?" Dean said, "My God, I'd better be!"

Like any professional performer, he had learned to rely upon nervousness and harness it for his purposes. Some comedy stars I've known have found the fear of flopping on stage overwhelming. Singers and musicians and actors look sympathetically at a pale, shaking comic. They require no more from the audience than some attention and applause, but the funny-man needs laughs or he's a disaster. Fine comedians suffer terribly from backstage terror, quite the worst I've seen. Yet that same awful fear came to their aid once they entered the spotlight. Suddenly the desire to take flight was transformed into energy and sparkle and snap. On a far higher level, the war heroes whose brave deeds have won the most glorious awards have described their own behavior in much the same way. Fear which might have mastered them became their servant.

HOW TO MASTER STAGE FRIGHT

How do you do it? Like acquiring any knack, you do it with a combination of simple acts. To ride a bike you combine balance, physical motions, persistence and the belief that it can be done. To turn pre-presentation nerves into controlled power requires an equally basic technique that is well within your capacity.

Prepare Everything That Can Be Prepared

Let's assume you have already prepared and rehearsed your speech. Now give yourself the confidence of knowing that you have considered everything else that could fail you and checked them too—lighting, sound, your face, hair and clothes, any changes in the audience that might affect your references to persons present, the availability of a drink if your mouth dries, all those details that can give you comfort and reassurance.

Some of this final preparation can be done during a banquet or conference while food is being served or others are speaking on the platform. I like to arrive at the venue early and look it over, see where I'm going to stand, get familiar with the setting and make sure I'll be visible and audible to everyone.

At a dinner you can choose a moment to slip out and check your appearance while the dessert is being served. Don't forget to smile in the mirror—that's when you spot the strand of spinach between your teeth.

Concentrate On How Good You Are

You know what you're going to say, you know how to say it, and it's very interesting, amusing, important, and altogether delightful. You are the best person to say it and they are lucky to have you here. Today you will win admiration and affection from everyone in the joint. Believe it. A little vanity boosts self-confidence.

This Is Not A Jury

Your audience is made up of individuals with whom you would have no difficulty in conversing. Now, instead of chatting to each person, one at a time, you're about to save a lot of time and chat to the whole bunch at once. It really is a mistake to regard an audience as a single entity sitting in hostile judgment. Remind yourself that none of these separate human beings could possibly scare you on their own. There is no reason to fear them collectively. Unless you are a conservative Republican facing a group of militant labor leaders, it's safe to assume that the natives are friendly.

Booze Is Like Success:
Both Are Great Until They Go To Your Head

You no doubt know your capacity for alcohol, but allow for its effect when mixed with the stimulation of excitement. At dinners, I always think the cocktail hour is a danger because there's usually no food in one's stomach and the booze can work faster. Since I dislike the idea of paying the French for designer water, I avoid Perrier and ask the waiter for "soda on the rocks". It sounds vaguely like a real drink.

Then it's safe to relax with the wine over dinner, as much as will produce a mild glow and no more. Hit the stuff hard and the hard stuff will hit back with slurred words, fluffed timing, forgotten names and fumbled notes.

Have no more to drink than you know will help you. Use it to loosen you up a little if that works for you but watch out for that over-solicitous wine waiter who keeps refilling your glass. It's so easy to quaff unthinkingly while simultaneously trying to pretend you're listening to the other speakers and mentally rehearsing your speech.

As for tranquilizers, they can calm a cough and reduce a tremor, but test your reaction to them on some earlier and relatively unimportant occasion. Don't use them for the first time before making a speech that matters. A Marketing Director of my acquaintance, worried about coping with a very vocal sales force, tried Valium for the first time. Feeling no different after taking two tablets, he swallowed three more. The salesmen, anticipating a top-class incentive scheme, greeted his appearance on the stage with prolonged cheers. He stood quietly and gazed at them fondly. Positive that he was about to proclaim great news, they cheered him again. Tears came to his eyes. "Thank you," he sobbed softly, "thank you so much." And he left the stage convinced that he had made the finest presentation of his life.

Shoot When You See the Whites Of Their Eyes

Some veteran speakers I know argue against eye contact. John Wade, a master magician and persuasive lecturer, advises inexperienced speakers not to look directly at anyone during a speech. He warns that by doing this you may seem to be speaking to this person alone and so embarrass them. Further, he believes that in engaging someone's eye unexpectedly, you risk being thrown off-balance should they wink or drop their eyes to the table.

He counsels speakers to look mostly towards the middle-distance, and also to move their gaze around the room, both near and far, without fixing upon any one person. Just occasionally, he suggests, you can focus on someone's eyes briefly, but otherwise you should keep your look wide, taking in the whole room and avoiding actual eye contact.

I really respect John but, in this one instance, I beg to differ. I believe lack of eye contact demonstrates lack of confidence. Looking sure of yourself is halfway to actually feeling the same way. And letting the audience see that you are secure is necessary to your control of the situation. If you feel anxiety, let it be a secret. Such feelings should be hidden. It's not hard to suppress the obvious outward signs of inner doubts: fussing with your clothes, constantly clearing your throat, easing a collar or jingling your loose change. I'm sure you're not planning to do any of that. But how do you feel about anyone who is talking to you but not looking you in the eye? Would you buy a used car from such a person? Or even a speech?

Another veteran speaker I know might agree with John Wade about eye contact. He needs glasses to see the audience so he used to leave them off when he went onstage. That way he could smile intimately at a blur, freed from the worry of seeing the odd unsmiling face in the crowd. Still another equally experienced orator would not agree. He strongly advises every novice, *"Do* look them straight in the eye." Opinion on this matter is clearly divided, so really it has to be your choice. From personal experiment you may already know what suits you better—looking squarely at your listeners or letting your gaze roam. Try both if you're still in doubt. But since this is the Monkhouse Method I'm advocating, let me promise you that a more assured and trustworthy impression comes to us from the speaker who is willing to look directly and frankly into our eyes. At any rate, please don't fix your focus on the floor or the ceiling. You may find everyone else doing the same, wondering what on earth is fascinating you so much.

Be Long-Winded Before You Speak

It's taught by singing teachers and in acting schools, but most performers pick it up naturally: it's easy, deep, regular breathing. It steadies the nerves, benefits the heart and, if you keep it up for life, you'll live until you die.

Filling the lungs evenly and slowly for a minute or two is an essential part of my technique for mastering nervousness. It helps to release tension in the neck and strain in the throat. And, as in most demanding situations, it reduces any feeling of panic. Actors waiting in the wings to make that first entrance use all sorts of quirky ways to burn off excess nervous energy—wriggling their hands, stretching, grimacing, bending—but the most common and most useful exercise is easy, steady, deep breathing.

Physically, it puts the world into perspective. The moments spent controlling your breathing are reassuring to the subconscious. The process is so basic to life and your personal security. Perhaps it reminds us that, no matter how stressful the task of making a speech, we'll still be breathing when it's over and done with.

If, while waiting to speak, you are unseen, outside a door or backstage, be uninhibited about how you relax yourself. Use the actors" tricks if they suit you—clenching and unclenching your hands, shaking your shoulders, arching your back—but keep those gentle, deep breaths going. If you're on a platform or at a table, sit back comfortably and deliberately slow down and deepen your breathing. And if it helps you to meditate on something, think about your purpose. Remember what result you want. Concentrate on your target. Discard inessential thoughts and focus on your motive. It's wonderful how this can awaken your sense of survival. And there you have my six-point strategy for marshalling the negative effects of stage fright and turning them into a positive support force. To recap:

Be Prepared!

Do your homework. Research, learn, revise and organize all you can about your subject, then write it down and rehearse it, then think about it and talk about it. Try it out on anyone willing to listen. Check every component of your presentation—your appearance, audience, audibility—leaving as little as possible to chance. All this preparation gives you something to be proud of, so:

Be Proud!

What you are offering to these people is top-quality merchandise—a splendid talk from a very worthwhile talker. Just bear in mind that you are sexy, lovable, amusing—and highly intelligent with it. Why else would you have this book?

Be Welcome!

The audience is not a monster that waits to destroy you, it is mostly composed of decent, friendly individuals. You know one or two may be lethargic, dim, worried or even in agony. That's their problem, not yours. The vast majority of the nice people listening and looking at a speaker actually like him.

Be Sober!

Use only enough alcohol to lift your morale as you prepare yourself—and no more.

Be Direct!

Find the friendliest faces in the audience and meet their gaze. When you've looked into enough interested eyes, you will know that this really is an agreeable audience, a pleasure to talk to.

Be Steady!

There's no need to rush breathlessly into a good speech. A few deep breaths and a quiet moment to review what you want your speech to achieve for you—and you're ready.

BUT WHAT ABOUT THE TREMBLES?

During auditions for a talent contest, I sat beside the producer watching up to 70 acts a day. He made notes on the back of each relevant application form, occasionally adding a cryptic V sign. One day I just had to ask.

"Is that a V for victory or the symbol for sticking up two fingers?"

"That, Bob, is a reminder that the performer in question is a vibrator," explained the producer. "Take that last singer. Good voice and unaffected by the tremors in her knees. But to conceal the shakes she had today, I'd have to get a cameraman with a bad hangover to tremble in tempo."

"So you wouldn't use her?"

"Wrong. No performer ever quivered through an entire show. The shaky period passes. It just means a bit of extra rehearsal perhaps, a few reassuring words and, if she's still rippling, no hand-mike. That's the most common give-away—the microphone with tremors."

The thought stayed with me. Had I ever been that agitated when called upon to perform? And how long did it last? And had I allowed it to be obvious to onlookers? Did my microphone have the shakes? And what could be done about it?

Then I remembered the twittering flutters that overcame me when I was called upon to speak at an adoption agency. My wife and I had applied to adopt a daughter and we had reached the stage where everything depended upon my making a convincing case to the committee. My God, did I have the shakes! I reckon I could have threaded a sewing machine while it was still running.

A few days earlier I had confided my fears to an old magician friend. "You have to handle so many magic props with precision, you can't afford to tremble. How can I conceal my shivers?"

He said, "In the first place, remember that nervousness doesn't show one-tenth as much as you feel. If you're slightly scared, you won't appear to be scared at all. And if you're very scared, you'll appear slightly scared. And if you're absolutely bloody terrified, you will only seem to be bothered."

If you suffer from physical shakes when you have to perform, you can take comfort from the truth of these two observations:

1. *Nobody ever quivered through an entire show*
2. *Nervousness doesn't display one tenth of itself*

And another thing—nobody gives a hoot. The audience couldn't care less if you fluff a few words and dab your napkin over your brow. They won't notice anything is wrong unless you throw up over the Master of Ceremonies or have cardiac arrest. If you doubt this, consider your own experience as a member of the audience. Think back. Can you recall one single speech that was affected by the speaker's evident fear? The fact is that you may have seen the occasional anxious speaker but, because it didn't really matter to you, it wasn't worth remembering. The odd exception might have been when you were emotionally involved with the speaker and sharing the tension on their behalf, but that's a special reaction you won't find in many audiences.

How then, can you conceal the outward manifestations of inward turmoil? Well, there are a few things you can do. And a few things you cannot do.

SIX WAYS TO COPE WITH NERVES

1. Take a tip from a veteran TV producer and don't hold a hand-mike if it's liable to shudder. Leave it on its stand.
2. Don't draw attention to your hands. If you must take a sip to drink, make it as sure and swift as you can—don't hold a glass of milk while it churns into butter.
3. Leave your notes on the table or the lectern where you can refer to them as necessary. If your eyesight demands closer scrutiny, raise them as briefly as possible and put them down again. When the air in the room is still but your papers are rattling in a gale then your cover is blown, so try not to hold them up too long or too close to the mike.
4. If one leg is trembling, shift your weight to the other. If both legs are trembling, move your feet back and lean forward with your hands on the table or grasping the lectern. Luckily for me, when I had to address the Adoption Panel, I could remain seated so my wobbly legs didn't show. I kept my hands gripping my knees so that I wouldn't be tempted to wring them piteously.
5. Avoid drinking anything with caffeine in it. Anyone prone to jumpiness can be overstimulated by tea or coffee or cola before a show. Kenny Everett, a comedian who sat beside me at a celebrity roast, admitted he was so nervous he didn't dare touch the coffee, then asked the waiter, "What's the right wine to go with fingernails?" But Kenny, the waiter and I were the only ones who knew he was tremulous. They all thought he was joking when he told them he was as insecure as an elephant's gynecologist.

   That was because Kenny could take his nervousness and make a gag about it and no-one suspected that he was genuinely tense. "Look at that hand shaking," he cried, stretching out a quivering arm. "I think people are having a sponsored walk across my grave!"
6. Don't let on! If you are naturally frank, you too may be tempted to tell the audience that you are nervous. That can work if you're a comedian like Kenny but I don't recommend it for anyone else, except as a rare deliberate device to gain sympathy for some purpose. The focus of your speech should

be upon its message and a confession of personal inadequacy won't help to get it across.

SHYNESS

I read that shyness can be inherited. I wanted to ask my parents if it ran in the family but I was too embarrassed to ask. Besides which, my mother was a very bashful woman. She wore a blindfold to change my diaper. I was breastfed through a rubber tube. From another room. My own modesty grew worse in adolescence. Even when I mentally undressed a girl, I stopped at her slip. Wait! Hold the jokes! Kidding aside . . .

Quite a few people, faced with the prospect of public speaking, feel they are naturally excluded from any success in the venture because they have discovered themselves to be socially shy. It ain't necessarily so. There is a remarkable Jekyll-and-Hyde effect which comes to the rescue of the generally demure. And I really do speak from personal experience.

Finding a Balance

Early in my show-business career I feared that my lack of complacency or arrogance would prove a handicap to my ambitions, so I assumed a more assured manner. Perceptive colleagues quickly deduced that I had a naturally retiring disposition and

encouraged me to fake self-assertion for the sake of my performances. Others mistook my artificially confident air for vanity and
disliked me for it. It took me years to find a balance between the
timidity of my real nature and the firm expression of personality
required of an aspiring star performer.

But you are not embarking upon a lifetime in the limelight.
You need only to overcome any reserve in your normal behaviour
long enough to take the stage, deliver your message and make
your impact. So what I have discovered in over forty years of hid-
ing my bushel and showing my light should be enough to help you
to do the same for twenty minutes.

How Bashful Celebrities Cope

More public figures tend towards shyness than you'd expect. One
powerful comedian who hurtles onto the cabaret floor with all the
subtlety of a hang-gliding flasher has a very private and self-
effacing nature. Commanding actresses like Anne Bancroft and
Teri Garr have appeared tongue-tied with self-consciousness
when interviewed. And a famous TV Host is an intensely secret
man who for many years clung to the privacy of a radio studio
rather than face the stare of an audience.

The list of such introverts in the public eye could run to half
a dozen pages. Perhaps you could compare us to stammerers
whose hesitant speech vanishes as soon as they sing the words.
There's something about being "on" that can turn shyness into
boldness as though an unsuspected alter ego were being let loose.
The blush of humility becomes the flush of freedom.

It's no surprise to psychologists that wall flowers blossom in
the warmth of attention. They will also tell you how often the
opposite holds true—that the life-and-soul-of-the-party can turn
into an agonized basket-case in front of a TV camera or a microphone. It's a simple inversion of role-playing and those of us who
draw in our horns in the presence of a few strangers can enjoy
an exhilarating release of constraint when we are given the right
to express ourselves in an authoritative situation.

Given a legitimate excuse to be aggressive, it can be goodbye
to Clark Kent. Of course, Superman's qualities include modera-
tion. Casting off shyness shouldn't be allowed to expose a raving

egomaniac bursting with blue jokes. That's no way to let the meek inherit the mirth.

Blushing

Don MacLean, one comic I know, said he took a course on "How to Stop Blushing": "They guaranteed one hundred per cent success but at the end of the course I still kept blushing. Then they sent me the bill and I went white."

If you tend to redden upon becoming the center of attention, it's worth thinking back to occasions when you have observed the same characteristic in others. Was your reaction anything worse than sympathetic amusement? There's something very likeable about a human weakness as endearing as a blush.

I recently attended an industrial show where a female television personality gave an impeccably professional presentation, linking the audio-visual display with interviews and voice-overs. She looked lovely and cool, in keeping with her TV image. Every man present admired her. Afterwards she joined the top table for dinner and stayed for my speech. I'd been on my feet for about three minutes when I cracked a slightly spicy joke about a topical headline. The gag hit her right on her elegant funnybone. She didn't just laugh, she erupted. The room was already laughing but, seeing the star's helpless heaving, the laughter doubled. Then she realized that the joke that had her rolling about was really rather rude. Her giggle came under control but there was nothing she could do to prevent the slow spread of pink suffusing her face. At which point, every man continued to admire her but also adored her.

Blushing is charming not only from a lovely woman. I've seen boxers blush and win affection by that involuntary reaction to a public compliment and you can't get much more masculine than the man who decked Muhammad Ali. Famous blushers include Arnold Schwarzenegger, and Joan Collins. I say, if you can do it, flaunt it.

Don't Worry About Competition

Those who suffer from shyness should never dwell upon the supposed superiority of other speakers on the program. It's hypothetical and self-defeating and, worse than either of those, it's fundamentally goofy.

There has never been a shortage of insecure performers who subscribed to this competitive concept. The great Al Jolson used to turn on the water taps in his dressing room so their gushing would drown the sound of applause given to fellow entertainers. Despite his massive star power Jolson's career waned as his ego ballooned, circumstances perhaps not unconnected. Two decades of public neglect were the price he paid for this, until he made his comeback when, though unchastened he was capable of such self-parody that the public could no longer withold its affection. Jolson joined Bing Crosby on radio and finally discovered it was as satisfying to be part of a good team as it was to fly solo.

Another American master of entertainment was Jack Benny and he adopted the good-team strategy early on. The huge and sustained popularity of his shows depended largely upon the contributions of support from Dennis Day, Phil Harris, Mary Livingstone and Eddie "Rochester" Anderson. Jack said, "People say the whole show's good and come back for more. But if people say only that Benny guy was good, they go someplace else looking for a better show." Better to be in a good company than a weak one. Let the entire cast shine; you share the reflection.

A Unique Maneuver

One famous radio and television star disliked making speeches, due only in part to his normal reticence. He was a slow student and took a disproportionate amount of time to memorize a script. Besides which he was always increasingly nervous as the time for a performance approached and hated the extra stress of having to be sociable right up to the last moment. But he'd been talked into attending a charity function and I was at the same top table when he pulled off the most cunning maneuver I'd ever seen. It's an inspired gag and well worth remembering for the day when you find yourself in similar circumstances.

There was only one speech ahead of his and it was given by a white-haired Catholic priest. There seemed no reason to expect anything out of the ordinary from this gentle, smiling septuagenarian but when he rose to his feet and began to talk, all heaven broke out. He was sly and witty and wonderful. The audience took him to their hearts and his slightest pleasantry had the room in an uproar. When the Father sat down to an ovation, the comic's expressive face was like granite. Then he was announced and stood up, warmly applauded by a rather exhausted and expectant crowd. His notes were in his fist. He waved them airily, nodded around the room and spoke.

"Just before we came in for dinner, the Father and I met in the men's room and you all know now how he is for a joke. He said to me, 'Wouldn't it be funny if we exchanged speeches and I did yours and you did mine?' So we did, and you've just heard mine. This is his and I'm not doing this load of rubbish—good evening!"

The Niels Bohr Superstition

According to that prodigious writer Isaac Asimov, there is a horseshoe fixed on the wall above the desk of the great Nobel Prizewinning physicist Niels Bohr. It has its open end up in the traditional way to catch good luck and hold it safely for the horseshoe's owner.

An American scientist visiting Bohr in Copenhagen asked him, "Surely a level-headed scientist like you, Professor Bohr, can't possibly believe that a horseshoe will bring you luck?" Chuckling, Bohr replied, "I believe no such thing, not at all. How could I give credence to such an absurd idea? However, I am told that a horseshoe will bring you luck whether you believe it or not."

If you put your trust in a rabbit's foot to see you through a public performance, I have another true story for you.

Tyrone Power was my guest star on the first TV variety show. As we read through the script I had written, I noticed a coin on a fine chain round his right wrist.

Tyrone's wife, Mai Zetterling, explained, "That's his lucky charm, that old thing—he's lost without it." Apparently the charm had been with him throughout his many films and he had a profound belief in its power to help him. "If I can't wear it on my wrist, I carry it in a pocket or some place," he told me.

The next evening we did the 90-minute live show. The audience cheered Tyrone Power's entrance and our crosstalk spot got good laughs. His other entrance was in a costume sketch, dressed as Zorro, the great swordsman. Just before his cue, Tyrone panicked. He told the floor manager, Ned Sherrin, "I've lost my chain, I must find it, otherwise I can't win out there!"

There was a hurried search but without success and, as I spoke his cue ("Am I not the world's greatest swashbuckler?"), Tyrone leaped from the balcony crying, "Not after I've buckled your swash!"

The sketch was a riot, but after the show, Tyrone remained inconsolable. "I was lousy in that scene; what else could I be? That charm is magical for me."

Then an impresario friend of his arrived, showering praise on us and adding, as an afterthought, "Your lucky chain, Ty dear boy, shall I have it mended for you?" He held out the coin on the broken chain.

The story was simple. In struggling to strap on his scabbard, Tyrone had snagged the chain and broken it. His dresser had picked it up and, knowing how the star prized its company, had put it into the pocket of Zorro's cloak before hurrying off to assist with another costume change. There was no time to tell Tyrone what he had done and afterwards he had forgotten all about it until it was time to gather up the discarded costumes.

Tyrone, who thought he was giving a poor performance because he hadn't got his lucky charm, was carrying it with him all the time. So the thing had no power. Or had it? His performance had been excellent. So it did work! But wait: he had *thought* his performance was lousy. His confidence was shaken and he had not enjoyed playing the sketch.

It's a curious little tale, don't you think? And the moral is: if you're a superstitious person and derive comfort from some lucky mascot, keep it with you—but don't depend on it so much that its loss will weaken your self-assurance. There's only one charm you should rely on—your own.

Technique
And Presentation

It's a pleasure to watch a good speaker. Yes, we listen to the words, the timing, the tones, to everything that is meant for us to hear. But the best of public declaimers are worth watching too. The man's stance is easy and commanding, his hands are used sparingly but with effect, and his head turns to everyone, including you. Every member of the audience seems important to him. No one is excluded from his range of attention.

In show business I have noticed how often amateur performers forget to spread the wealth, sometimes limiting the extent of their appeal to a narrow section of the audience. You may have suffered the same apparent lack of interest from a speaker who, though intending to address everybody, neglects your side of the auditorium. There you sit on his blind side, nary a glance coming your way, feeling more and more restless and resentful. A first-class speech may be going to waste, all because of the speaker's inconsiderate posture.

You can avoid this by matching your physical attitude to the confident manner you are adopting mentally. Stand, sit, or move with pride. People understand body language so let your body's attitude speak for you. Try rising to your full height and then easing back comfortably, legs slightly apart, head back so that your voice can penetrate clearly. Let your head move naturally, taking in every aspect of the audience area. Each person looking at you deserves a look back, just a glance now and then that tells them you know and care that they are there. Don't let someone's scowl throw you; it might be a frown of intense concentration. Concentrate, as you survey the room, on giving everyone a share of yourself.

HOW NOT TO MAKE A GOOD IMPRESSION

Have you ever attended a function where the principal speaker seems to think he's in the dark until he stands up? I've seen him yawn, scratch, stare vacantly into space, ransack his nose, stare down grouchily at his notes, eat like a junkyard dog, guzzle his wine, ignore the conversation of his neighbors, and generally give the entire room a lesson in unrelieved boorishness.

But as soon as he's introduced, Mr. Hyde disappears and up stands good Dr. Jekyll.

Forget it, the audience caught the show right from the start and they know a phoney when they see one. This fellow's mistake was that he just didn't think about being on display until now. He's really not much use to us except as an object lesson. Whether you're nervous or confident, your performance begins with your first entrance and your image starts to take shape in the minds of the audience. Be yourself, by all means, but let your best side show. Let them say, "You can tell he's a gentleman by the way he behaves", or, if you're female, "Her manner is so charming, a real lady." We may not all have good breeding but at least we can conduct ourselves so that we get the benefit of the doubt.

PROJECTION

You breathe normally about 18 times a minute—that's 26,000 breaths a day—and it's all controlled by a breathing center conveniently located at the base of your brain and at the top of your spinal cord. This center coordinates all the muscular movements necessary for your respiration. If it goes wrong, only an iron lung can do the job.

Your lungs are enclosed in a flexible box. The sides of the box are your ribs, linked at the back to your backbone and at the front to your breastbone. Your neck is on top and your diaphragm is the base. You use your lungs like a bellows which contains a very elastic sponge attached to its sides. Why am I telling you all this? Because it is your speech-making machinery and you can do a better job if you remember how it works.

Try this: Put your hand flat against your diaphragm. That's just below your ribcage. Now, without raising your shoulders, take a deep breath. You should feel the diaphragm expanding. If not, try it again, concentrating on making that muscle swell against your palm. Okay, now hold your breath in for a beat and then shout, "Hallelujah!" while exhaling. Use your throat as a tunnel and let the word ride on the air expelled by your diaphragm. You'll be surprised at how far your "Hallelujah" will carry without straining your throat muscles.

Now try expanding your diaphragm by sniffing an imaginary gas leak. You'll feel the muscle respond to each intake of air as you sniff, sniff again, don't exhale yet, sniff, sniff again, until your lungs are filled, now let it all out with another effortless "Halle-lujah!" By now everyone within earshot will be convinced that you've Finally Seen the Light. If you want to substitute a word of your own for this exercise, please do. You might try "Hosannah in the highest" or, if religious ecstasy is not your style, "Hail her-esy!" Just practice with a breathy sort of word that doesn't close your lips or impede the outward passage of air.

THE STEVE ALLEN CREDO

America has enjoyed its *Tonight Show* on TV since 1954. Notable as the first unscripted comedy program to attain national pop-ularity, it made a star out of host Jack Paar and, since 1961, a multi-millionaire of Paar's successor, Johnny Carson. But the first and most feckless star of the show began it on radio and pio-neered a new sort of extemporaneous humor; he was the versatile Steve Allen.

Allen didn't invent the studio audience interview but he was the first to conduct relaxed conversations with members of the public and simultaneously create original and funny jokes on the spot. People marvelled that he was able to go on TV with the min-imum of preparation and produce 1 hour 45 minutes of sponta-neous, amusing chatter for five nights a week. But Allen saw nothing unique in what he could do.

We're told by psychologists and philosophers that we use only a small part of our potential powers, and an example of this is the way in which we talk every day. Allen was confounded by the surprise expressed at a man able to stand up in front of others and talk to them without a script when, he reasoned, everyone does exactly the same thing every hour of every day they are in human contact.

When you walk into your office or a restaurant or a baker's shop, you didn't have to hover anxiously outside rehearsing what you would say. And when you bump into a neighbor or greet a friend, you have no need of previous planning to hold a conver-sation. You employed the natural human gift of communication through language. So, if you can talk at all, your next step is simple—learn to talk to more than one person at a time. All that requires, according to Allen, is experience. The more you do it, the easier it gets.

"The trick," wrote Allen, "is in being relaxed enough to speak on the air as easily as you do in the living room. Experience is the key. . . . I do not feel that the ability to make chatter on stage is unusual or noteworthy." That's what Steve Allen believes. Okay, but he can afford to believe that. He is a born talker and a seasoned inventor of verbal comedy. "A natural golfer can afford to believe that anyone with the coordination to walk and chew gum at the same time should be able to sink a putt under stress. We, the rest of us, know that it isn't so easy.

But there is merit in Allen's argument, and a wider application which includes amateur performers. It is true that we all communicate each day without fear of failure. Of course, certain persons may make us more tense than others. We may feel nervous when we have to address someone in authority like the bank manager, the tax inspector or the doctor. But it's also true that, just as familiarity breeds contempt, so does experience bring a reduction of anxiety. This is certainly relevant for people planning to improve their public speaking:

You should expand your opportunities to use your normal powers of conversation, voice your opinions and convey your feelings. Seek situations where you can feel relaxed and welcome, whether it's a club, pub or family party, and set out to be heard. If your thoughts need to be organized before you can feel secure when expressing them, write them out—but don't use notes when you speak. Exercise your memory instead. A professional entertainer may be at ease speaking off the cuff but his "notes" are still part of his equipment, familiar to him from repetition and invisible to his audience. So practice and keep on practicing until, like Steve Allen, you wonder why people think you're such a brilliant speaker.

PUT SIGNPOSTS ON YOUR SCRIPT

As you lay out the principal part of your completed notes, give yourself every visual assistance so that you can easily find your place and recognize the headings. I work from key words written in heavy plain black capitals for the factual material and highlight my joke ideas with a green fluorescent marker. Why green? Too often I have given myself written reminders in red or blue, only to find that the podium is illuminated with lights of red or blue. The writing became invisible. So far no lunatic has put me in a green spot.

Peter Sellers marked his scripts with all kinds of instructions to himself—arrows and squiggles and little loops that somehow reminded him of what he'd planned to do with pauses and emphases. The letter Z meant "pause in thought", I remember; though I don't remember why.

I watched a charmingly diffident speaker giving a speech written by me and my late partner, Denis Goodwin, and saw big purple polka-dots down the left margin. The speaker put his index finger on each one as he spoke, moving it down to the next big dot as he dealt with the previous paragraph. Sometimes he changed hands but he never lost his place or stumbled over a word.

I recommend trying this. It can be comforting, after delivering a minute or so of your stuff facing directly to the room, to look down at your script and find a big, friendly number or letter or cross that you put at the start of the next thing you have to say. Once you've found a personal method of marking your words, practice with it. When it feels comfortable to you, trust it. After all, you will have done the marking in tranquility and rehearsed with it to your satisfaction. It would be unwise to abandon good advice when it's your own.

CONCEAL A BULKY SCRIPT

If the middle and main part of your script is long and detailed, taking up many pages, try not to show it to the audience. You'll scare them. The sight of a speaker mounting the dais hefting a bundle of paper that could choke a hippo is intimidating. In a case like this, I'd break with my own experience-trained habit of never letting go of my words lest some pest pinches them, put the massive script on the lectern earlier on and step into the limelight empty-handed. Then no-one can know how long you're going to be.

SAYING IT SIMPLY

The language of your speech may be dictated by scientific, technical, historical, industrial, political, educational, statistical or other professional jargon. But I would urge you to simplify and personalize such material, even when addressing an audience of experts familiar with the specialist terms.

The success of experts on TV depends upon their mastery of communication. They humanize inhuman facts. They break up complicated details into short sentences and use simple words wherever they can replace long ones. When a statistician tells us that "twenty per cent of the population in the New York Metropolitan Area did not receive dental care in 1989", he is explaining himself less well than if he said, "One in five New Yorkers didn't see a dentist last year." Even if he'd been addressing an audience of dentists the basic rules of communicating still apply. One way is dull, the other isn't.

Gobbledegook

The signs of businessmen's banality are all too paralyzingly apparent. Eloquence departs as does simple English. Parameters replace limits. An alternative cannot be offered by itself, it has

62

to be a viable alternative. Your company cannot grow, it must have growth potential. God preserve us from Chairmen who embark upon an "overview of our dynamic posture in pursuant days."

Give the Audience a Chance

There is a very simple rule about local and regional accents. If the audience has an unfamiliar accent, then so have you. Please slow down.

Between 2,000 and 3,000 languages are spoken throughout the world, not including the ones used by teenagers. When the English-speaking people go abroad without any command of the foreign tongue, they tend to shout very slowly at the natives as if talking to a deaf person: "Por favor, camarero, uno beero and duo sweet sherryo for the senoras!" It's idiotic but it often seems to work. Of course, the instinctive wisdom in this behaviour is slowing down and increasing the clarity of the words.

A Brooklynite in Houston soon learns to speak steadily and distinctly in shops and hotels to overcome the barrier of his unfamiliar accent. So it should appear obvious to a Boston, Massachusetts, Manager who comes to address a Helena, Montana, Sales Force that he should make allowances for his regional use of English. Not surprisingly, however, other considerations often take precedence and the problem of his alien accent gets forgotten. And if the visiting speaker warms to his subject, he may even speed up until he becomes unintelligible. So, please, whenever you are due to speak to a group of people who sound funny to you, assume that you sound funny to them.

Underline key words and emphasize them, especially if they contain vowels which undergo a local distortion as you travel around the country. You may even choose to make a light-hearted and self-deprecatory reference to your own way of pronouncing English.

TO BE OR NOT TO BE— WHAT WAS THE QUESTION?

A Shakespearean actor has every right to his pre-show jitters. If he blows his lines, he blows his reputation. The opera singer is fully entitled to a little tension in the wings—her audience knows the libretto as well as she does. But the speaker need have no such fear. You are not reciting deathless prose or famous poetry. If you are ever stuck, you can switch to other words. If you forget the exact phrase you intended to use, you can replace it with another. No-one but you will ever know.

That's the handy thing about language—it's full of redundancies and superfluities. There's always another way of putting things. So take comfort in the fact that you are not required to be line perfect, only comprehensible. When precise memory fails you, fluency will come to your aid. The most important thing is, know what you're talking about. As long as you know the meaning of your message, the words you use to convey it can be subject to alteration even as you draw breath to speak them.

So there's never any need to fear disaster because a particular word or line in your prepared text escapes you. The audience doesn't know what's supposed to come next. Just concentrate on meaning and the exposition will follow.

THE CANNON'S ROAR TECHNIQUE

A Director I know loves to tell the tale of an amateur actor who is given one line to speak in an historical play. His one line is:

"Hark! I hear the cannon's roar!"

All day long he rehearses the line—"Hark! I hear the cannon's roar!"—in the bath, over breakfast, on the bus, during working hours, tea and lunchbreaks, all the way home, watching TV, lying in bed at night—"Hark! I hear the cannon's roar!"—week after week until the night of the performance. He stands confidently on the stage, awaiting his cue. Just as the moment arrives for him to speak his line—"Hark! I hear the cannon's roar!"—the stage manager gives the signal for the sound effect and there's an enormous backstage bang. And the actor says:

"What the hell was that?"

And the moral is a good one for public speakers to bear in mind. Whatever you say is in context. Your words are never isolated from the setting in which they are spoken. You should always be conscious of what surrounds you in case it reflects upon what you plan to say. Has some previous speaker pre-empted one of your ideas? If so, should you drop it? Perhaps you can retain it with a reference to its repetition—"As the Chairman has already said this evening, and it's a point worth repeating . . ." Unlike our surprised actor whose line was memorized blindly, never forget why and where and when your words will be delivered. Then, when your speech is ended and you sit down, at least no one will mutter,

"What the hell was that?"

FOUR POINTS TO PONDER

1. If dramatic inflections and motions do not come naturally to you, don't worry about it. Remember what William L. Shirer wrote about the Mahatma: "Gandhi was not an orator. He scarcely raised his voice and made no gestures." If the man who inspired a nation with his words had no need of histrionics, neither do you.

2. Your hosts may be reluctant to tell you how long—or how short—they'd like your speech to be. Find out for your own sake.

3. A speech is easier to write than any other written work because errors don't show. The audience will only hear it once and they can't spot mistakes in spelling or punctuation. Few people speak in correctly structured sentences. Why should you? You can be as natural on the page as you want to be on your feet.

4. Don't rewrite your speech immediately after your first draft. You're too closely involved with what you've just written and haven't the perspective necessary to edit it. Leave it for a day or two, longer if convenient. You'll return to it with a much more critical eye than would have been possible before.

The Corporate Speechwriter

This is really a section for the busy executive to consider. Although happy to write his own material, and reasonably satisfied with the results, he may reach a phase in his career where he no longer has enough time to devote to preparing all the speeches he has to deliver. As he moves up the corporate ladder, this becomes a more pressing problem, compounded by the fact that he is now addressing higher-level audiences than before and the importance of getting everything just right is more crucial than ever, and more difficult to achieve.

If this is happening to you, now is the time to look around your organization in search of a writer. It is entirely possible that you already have someone in the company who could write your speeches just as well as, if not better than you.

Unused or misused writing talent is all too common in large corporations. Your advertising copywriters or house magazine feature writers may be fully stretched doing what they do, but occasionally such specialists turn out to have the additional and different skills necessary for writing good speeches. Your Public Relations Director is writing or causing to have written all sorts of material about your business. Here again there just might be a person of suitable talent to write a speech for you, someone who only needs to be briefed on the message you want to convey in order to compose an effective pitch. Perhaps all they need is the chance to try.

Dangers

Finding an able writer who is eager to show the required qualities is hard. Misusing that writer is easy. You could do it by having someone else brief the writer when it's your personality he or she needs to capture, your natural style that must be communicated on the page. And when the script is delivered, you can have it edited by cautious aides, who will blue-pencil every trace of daring and dash. Once wit and originality have been replaced with commercial cliches, safety will be re-established and a dozen dull pages assembled by unimaginative committee can arrive on your desk.

Don't Just Read It, Speak It

But let's assume you give your time and trouble to a promising writer and, under your personal instruction, a script comes directly into your hands. How should you judge it? Certainly not by reading it as you would a feature article in *USA Today*. There's a considerable difference in writing for the eye and writing for the ear. Give it voice. Read it aloud. Tape it and play it back. Its faults and virtues will reveal themselves at once. Your own version of Hemingway's alarm system will let you know whether you have gold in your grasp or crap in your lap. And if it falls short beyond redemption, what then? Where do you find a better speechwriter?

Aside from personal recommendation from successful corporate speakers or top executives you trust, you might consider advertising. A businessman I know put an ad in *The Wall Street Journal*, had five replies, tried all five with the same assignment, found a winner and has hired him ever since.

Calling In The Professionals

If you can't spare the time and effort for all this, perhaps you can afford to throw money at the problem, at which point the best professional organizations will taken an interest. There are just a few companies which provide the know-how for industrial shows plus speechwriters. These experts understand the subtleties of spoken persuasion, and they will not be scared to argue with you when they think your ideas are wrong. They spend their working lives dealing in the techniques of communication. And their best writers can put your voice into print. That's what your speeches need, that unique tone which is recognizably yours, not a cacophony of false notes. Just as you would detect an uncharacteristic line coming from the mouth of the President, so your audience can sense your use of phrases alien to your style. It's like Segovia playing a wrong note.

These service companies can also produce your presentations and provide equipment to help you, such as automatic cueing devices and transparent lecterns, so if this possibility appeals to you, check them out.

Whose Voice?

I'm not suggesting you accept whatever opinions a professional writer offers. Let his arguments prevail on their own merit, and always show his completed script to your colleagues or your spouse to test their reactions. A good speech should be a collaborative creation in which only one person is heard loud and clear—and that's you.

Say It With Humor

The most popular and engaging method of beginning any address is humor. It's that perfectly judged and confidently delivered opening line that both grasps and relaxes the audience. They know they are safe with you. With one *appropriate* quip you have told everyone within earshot that you know what you're doing. You're in charge.

I emphasize the word appropriate. Believe me, I'm not asking you to become a comedian. The profession's overcrowded enough as it is. The point I am making is that humor has to be handled with care if it is to succeed. Each joke or amusing remark is right for certain occasions and no good for others. Sorting out what can go where, and why, is one of my principal aims in this chapter.

WHERE TO BEGIN

Anything can be grist for your mill when the time comes to plot a speech. An attractive phrase, fractured proverb, epigram or verse, a new twist to an old anecdote, an ironic news item or amusing misprint, puns, tall tales, a movie wisecrack or a cartoon caption. The more you add to your collection of such basic material, the more you will have to choose from.

Does this mean you need to buy joke books—those comic anthologies which have millions of quips and quotes in them? Well, you can try, but the trouble with joke books is that they tend to ruin both your appetite for humour and your sense of what is funny. To wade through a thousand jokes you can't use to find one that you can is brain-pickling. Of course, it may be worthwhile. By doggedly searching the dozens of speakers' handbooks available in the shops and libraries, you will occasionally strike gold. But most of the time it's like swallowing oysters. A dozen can be delightful, but a hundred would be horrendous.

Adopt a discipline when you read any treasury of jokes. Limit yourself to a few pages at a time, perhaps a quarter of an hour and no more, three times in any one day. Otherwise your judgment will break down.

HOW TO CHECK OUT EVERY JOKE YOU USE

This brings me to a crucial part of the joke-selection process. To have any chance of success on the night, every joke you include in your script must pass the following four-point test.

1. *Do you think it's funny?*
2. *Can you say it confidently and with comfort?*
3. *Is there any danger of offending anyone?*
4. *Will they understand and appreciate it?*

The answer has to be yes to all four questions. And the cardinal rule of my very first TV producer should always apply: *When in doubt, cut it out.* I'm all in favor of well- chosen saucy lines. They are usually the loudest laughs. But it must always be the audience that determines the bounds of good taste for you. In selecting your racier humor, you have to anticipate just how they will react. Let's now run through the four points of the test.

1. Do you *think it's funny?*

This first question is about your personal taste. You will always deliver a funny line better if you genuinely like it. If, on the other hand, it puts you in stitches every time you even think about it, you had better not risk telling it in a fit of giggles. In fact, send it to me. Any joke that funny is one I'd like to put in my act.

2. Can you say it confidently and with comfort?

You may yourself have heard an inexperienced speaker who's been told a joke the night before and is determined to jam it into his speech regardless of whether or not it suits his style, appearance, personality, or ability.

I recall a 22-year-old salesman rising to propose a toast to a banquet hall full of middle-aged grocers and their wives. He launched into a repetitious anecdote about a second honeymoon which I recognized at once with some degree of horror. It required a mastery of accents, and he hadn't got it. It needed the authority of mature years and he hadn't got that either. It needed timing, expressive gestures and practiced articulation for the tongue-twisting punchline. The poor fellow was bereft of the lot. But those grocers and their spouses were very kind to him. They just ignored him. I've known audiences that would have lynched him.

3. Is there any danger of offending anyone?

There is always a distinct possibility that, whatever you say, you risk offending somebody somehow. Even a minister's sermon can upset the sensibilities of his flock. The tough part of this question is knowing how to apply it.

Should you play so safe that you omit even the mildest critical comment, the least suggestive wink, the gentlest leg-pull? That policy sounds a bit wet—and could leave you sounding extremely dry. So let's agree that any speaker wishing to employ freedom of expression enlivened with wit must inevitably accept the risk of annoying a listener or two.

Watch out, in particular, for jokes which touch on:

Physical appearance
Political bias
Religion
Disabilities

First, PHYSICAL APPEARANCE. The Chairman and the guest speaker were close friends and had already joked in private about the former's outstanding feature, his big nose. But the audience wasn't in on this joke. When the speaker said, "Yesterday the Chairman celebrated his fiftieth birthday. If it weren't for that nose he'd be 14 hours older!"—nobody laughed.

They were embarrassed for the Chairman whose huge honker they had noted but politely ignored. The speaker then compounded his error. He had a second joke prepared on the nasal topic, one he should have instantly dropped, but the booze had dulled his judgment so on he plunged: "That nose is so big, he has to get a mining permit to pick it!" There was a silence you could have used to freeze peas. The message reached the speaker's brain but instead of recognizing his mistake and switching subjects, he fell into defiant panic and tried to save the day with, "But don't worry, he's having a nose job . . . ROTO ROOTER'S GOT THE CONTRACT!" Groans, calls of "Sit down!," sarcastic applause . . . and the wretched speaker subsided. He'd made an easily avoided gaffe.

Of course, big noses can get laughs. Jimmy Durante's schnozzola, Bob Hope's ski-snoot, Barbra Streisand's beak, Barry Manilow's snorkel—they've all garnered their share of affectionate mirth.

But these are public personalities who have put themselves simultaneously both in the limelight and on the firing range. They are legitimate targets for the comics to snipe at. Private citizens are not.

Jibes about celebrities are usually acceptable, but making a crack about the managing director's warts could be hazardous to your wealth. Leave such insults to the full-time comedians whose stock-in-trade they are. Even the wittiest of personal remarks about physical appearance can sound bitter or bitchy, so rule them out.

Second, POLITICAL BIAS. Unless you are very well known for your political stance and therefore expected to make partisan remarks, stick to a fair-minded and reasonable position if political issues must be dealt with. If you want to use a loaded joke about a Democrat, balance it with another about a Republican.

Third, RELIGION. Yes, there are some lovely anecdotes with a religious setting and they're well worth employing. But once you wander into the churchyard in search of smart jokes, you're also in a minefield. You'll find some useful and safe suggestions under "Laughing on Religious Grounds" later in this book. If you decide to explore further, beware sensitive souls.

Fourth, DISABILITIES. Please forgive me for stating the obvious. Of course you already know that handicaps are not funny. But while it's easy to avoid the obviously tasteless reference to blindness or polio, there are some less apparent pitfalls.

Last Christmas, in a single comedy show I counted seven jokes that could have caused personal distress. The straight man told the comic, "You're a cretin," the comic told him about the bus conductor and a passenger with no arms and one leg ("Hop on, mate, you look 'armless"), and we suffered comical wheezes about a leper, rape, black Jamaican stupidity, male and female homosexuality, and even child pornography.

The fact that this material had been written, submitted, accepted, paid for, rehearsed, memorized, performed to a laughing studio audience and then televised—all this could give it a spurious legitimacy. An unwary viewer with a forthcoming speech to prepare might then be tempted to use one of the cleverer lines, thinking that if it was acceptable on the screen, it would be acceptable from the platform. He doesn't see the post from outraged viewers piled on the TV producer's desk or hear the complaints jamming the telephone switchboards. So he cracks a little joke about the company doctor—"He told me I was a schizophrenic but I'm of two minds about it"—and wonders why a lady in the audience has started to weep. Schizophrenia, alas, is a tragic condition and no joke to a parent whose son is suffering from an advanced form of it. This exact situation actually happened, and I use it as a general warning to look carefully at your finished speech and be prepared to censor it.

4. Will they understand and appreciate it?

If you're going to face an unfamiliar bunch of faces, research is vital. Assuming you know roughly who they are in general, you need information about their age group, average social position, expectations from a speaker, etc. One master of post-prandial dissertation uses a lovely opening line:

"I asked for a complete list of everyone present, broken down by age and sex . . . but, looking round, I see most of us are."

Once you have an approximate profile of your listeners, you also need to know of any outstanding personalities in the room who might warrant inclusion, the identity of any possible hecklers and, if the occasion is a regular event, how previous speakers have fared. All these clues are a guide to the degree of subtlety or simplicity you can employ.

It isn't difficult to adjust the accessibility of your meaning by varying the way you express it. You do it every time you speak to your spouse, children, to tradesmen, colleagues, waiters, shop assistants, the doorman or the boss. You get your meaning across to each of them by talking in a way they can best understand.

It's the same with audiences. Take the time and trouble to figure out who they are and what they are capable of grasping quickly and easily. If your most subtle joke misfires because the audience doesn't get it, it's really not their fault, it's yours. You assessed their powers of comprehension wrongly.

Using The Four Checks

Okay, our sample joke is on test. It's one from a beloved little comedian widely regarded as one of the funniest men ever to stand at the top table and talk:

"My friends, if I may I'd like to include a personal note— today is my 40th wedding anniversary. (*Applause*) Thank you, it's a great occasion for me and a time to mark with generosity so I asked my wife to name anything she'd like to have, and I would buy it for her. I said, 'You want a Rolls Royce, I'll give you a Rolls Royce.' She said, 'I don't want a Rolls Royce.' I said, 'Name it, it's yours—you want me to get you a diamond pendant, a penthouse on the Riviera, a yacht, I'll get it for you.' She said, 'I don't want any one of those things.' I said, 'All right, what *do* you want?' She said, 'I want a divorce.' I said, 'To tell you the truth, I wasn't thinking of spending that much.'"

Now apply the test. Do you think it's funny? Can you say it confidently and with comfort? Is there any danger of offending anyone? Will they understand and appreciate it? If it passes all those questions, the joke has lift-off.

THE NUTS AND BOLTS OF LAUGHTER

Most of the successful public speakers I know are strongly aware of joke construction. Just a few have a flair for instant comic invention while the majority have simply developed their feel for what makes a joke funny; when they build the humorous parts of their speeches they do so with great care. It's worth your time to do the same.

Once you have a grasp of the engineering principles, you will be able to assemble the components of a joke more easily, because you know its key words and vital stresses, you'll remember each joke better and deliver it more expertly. What's more, this enhanced sense of joke construction will help you to assess the value of other people's jokes and improve upon them. This is particularly true of that oh-so helpful amusing opening. Take these first words used by the American comedian Alan King:

"Ladies and Gentlemen, it gives me great pleasure and no money to be here today."

The secret of that line lies in the brevity with which one's formal expectations are aroused by its first half and then exploded by the disrespectful bluntness of its second half. By using the normal opening words to disarm the audience's anticipation of a gag—"Ladies and Gentlemen"—and continuing with the instantly recognizable cliche"—"It gives me great pleasure"—the mind of every listener is already moving ahead to complete the familiar sentence—"to be here today"—but, wham, in come those three intrusive words, placed not at the end of the phrase but within it—*"and no money* to be here today".

How Does A Joke Work?

I've heard it said that dissecting a joke is like dissecting a frog—the thing dies in the process and its insides are discouraging to any but the scientific mind. Don't you believe it!

No magician could perform a trick without having total knowledge and control of its physical and psychological elements. It's the same with a joke. When you speak the words that make up a joke and the people laugh, you've accomplished exactly what a good conjuror does but with one magical addition. The laugh.

Here's an opening line from one speaker who had sat through a slow formal banquet and two rambling speeches:

"Mr. Chairman, Ladies and Gentlemen, what a great dinner. If I'd known it was going to run this long I'd have *bought* the tux."

Why is it funny? Because of its construction. Rephrase the same idea and it falls apart. Just as Alan King's line required its comedy tucked inside it, this line depends upon the way in which he shaped it. If Alan had said, "It gives me great pleasure to be here today *but no money,*" the comedy would have been lost. The phrasing, "I wouldn't have hired this suit if I'd known the dinner was going to run this long," might have won a smile or two but the punch would have been missing.

That's not to say there's only one way to put over a comic idea. Once you've got the nuts and bolts of a joke, there may be a dozen ways to arrange them. It's just a matter of finding the pattern of words that suit your style.

Punchlines

A punchline is exactly that—a line that should pack a punch. So make sure you know it. If you are at all uncertain of the exact phrasing of the tag, either drop the joke or have a written note of the payoff where you can easily see it. Don't paraphrase. And please don't fade out as you reach that big finish. Give it all you've got and it will give you all it's got.

COLLECTING GOOD MATERIAL

The Card File

The first time I ever saw a card index used for comedy was when I delivered a radio script to the headline comedian in a hit show for which I had been told to write a funny sketch in which the star would play a Viking called Eric the Red.

His first line came after he was asked, "Are you Olaf the Black?' to which he replied, "No, I'm a Norse of a different color." That's how bad the sketch was. The star read through it without smiling. The silence in his dressing room was awful. I tried to brighten the gloom by saying, "I saw the show last week and you were brilliant, so naturally funny," to which he replied, "How old are you?" I told him I was twenty. "No wonder you don't know any better," he grunted. Then he pulled out a drawer, removed a long cardboard box, took out a handful of index cards and dealt them out on his dressing table.

"Some men are born comics," he said as he slid the cards around like a fortune-teller. "I am not one of them, though I've often wished I were. I have no natural genius for the art. Fortunately for me, that's not necessary, though it would have made my working life a shade less difficult. I am essentially a studied comic. His beautifully shaped hands hovered briefly over a final arrangement of the cards. "There," he sighed, "I've written my monologue."

What the star had done was a trick I've often used since. He'd had hundreds of short jokes typed separately onto cards, each with a reference heading. To assemble a seven-minute patter spot for the radio show, he took a handful at random and shuffled them around into a sequence. It needed very little invention to link the gags with some sort of lunatic logic.

It looked easy but, like so many easy achievements, it was based upon past industry. He had spent years travelling all over the USA working in jazz joints and vaudeville, touring the music halls and cabarets, reaching fame on radio—and all the while he was collecting jokes. Never without a notebook, he had jotted down every funny remark he'd overheard, every smart retort, even

77

clever captions from newspaper cartoons. When he could afford to hire a typist, the entire library of laugh lines was transcribed onto 3 x 5 inch cards and the store in the cardboard box continued to grow. It was just a matter of getting the habit and keeping it up.

Comedy For the Ear Is Not For the Eye

Some of the best performable comedy looks dreary in print. If a critic wants to sneer at a sitcom on TV, he only has to quote the "funny" dialogue. What played perfectly well the night before looks pathetic in the morning paper. Conversely, written humor which reads delightfully and sells books is usually hapless stuff to perform. You get a feeling for the difference, and that feeling gets stronger with each successful choice—and each misjudgment. Yes, once again, just when you need a shortcut, the job needs hard work and experience. But, saints be praised, it can be a lot of fun, and when the audience rewards your effort and perception with their laughter, it's a great feeling.

Classify and Reclassify

As your card index begins to grow, classify each entry with the information you will need for accurate retrieval. A gag may have more than one possible use, so use plenty of cross-indexing. Take this line about politicians: "The only time they're telling the truth is when they call each other liars." The first heading for that might be "Politics"—but what if you need a line about "Truth" or "Elections" or "Local Government" or "Summit Meeting"? The more you cross-index the more your range will grow.

Collecting on Your Investment

Finally, how does the card file pay off? Here's one scenario. You've agreed to speak at the local Rotary. There's a shopping list to be prepared before you browse through your file: where are you speaking, who will be there, who else is speaking, names of previous or present guests, the topics you might cover (unusual weather, current local and national events, etcetera), the range of your speech and its main theme, and so on.

Now you can dip into your file and take out every relevant card.

Spread the cards out and begin to form an order. Soon a pattern of possible use will become clear. There will be an embarrassment of riches and you can start the process of selection and rejection. Remember, these card ideas are here to support your speech, not to invade or distort it.

First, a valuable line for your opening, now perhaps a good one about the parking difficulties in the neighborhood, then you'll be into your main theme and will need no laughs for a while, but a popular anecdote to amplify the point might help, and here's the very one. An apt quotation might lead you into a summary of your serious points, then a warm-hearted way of expressing your thanks to conclude, yes, this card will fit, and so ends an engaging 20 minutes.

The cards have done their job, arranged like friendly milestones along the path of your speech. And as their number increases over the years, they will repay the public speaker's industry over and over again.

"A Funny Thing Happened on the Way Here . . ."

It's a reliable standby you've heard from hundreds of patter comedians over the years. Often the funny thing that the comic says happened on the way here isn't all that funny and obviously didn't happen. However, nothing surprises in comedy unless it works and there's never been a simpler opening line for a comic—or for a speaker. So let's take up a few paragraphs to see what value it can have for you.

Topicality

This familiar formula adapts itself naturally to headlines, When the MTA of New York City went on strike, one comic opened his act by saying, "A funny thing happened to me on the way here—I caught a bus." It scored a big laugh purely on its topicality. If all the morning papers carry the same front page story and it's not tragic, try fitting it into the "Funny Thing" formula to see if it gives you a smart opening.

Local Interest

Here's where the phrase can be based on truth. On the way from the railway station to the banquet hall where he was due to speak, a speaker found himself in the company of a very chatty cabdriver. "This is Broadway," he announced, "famous for always being dug up. In fact, it's a miracle there's no workmen digging it up today." The speaker had his opener: "A funny thing happened on the way here. I drove down Broadway without stopping for roadwork." Applause!

Mood-setting

It's possible to use the "Funny Thing" device as a lighthearted introduction to a serious theme. One speaker did so in a charming speech to college students. He rose to thank the college President for his introduction and then said, "I've never really believed all those comedians on the radio and on the stage who begin by saying, 'A funny thing happened to me on the way here today' because nothing funny has ever happened to me on the way to a public appearance. Never! Until today!" The teachers and students laughed at that and settled down, happy with the realization that they were listening to an able speaker.

Then he went on with his story of how the wind had blown his hat off his head and into the road, a daring boy had run after it and barely managed to scoop it out of the path of a truck, only to trip and fall on top of the hat. The speaker's rueful expression as he showed us all the battered black hat was funny and endearing. Immediately he used the tale as an example of the pitfalls awaiting those who are over-eager to oblige and enlarged his theme as he encouraged us all to do good without becoming do-gooders.

It was a fine and serious talk but it might not have secured our rapt attention without its engaging beginning. The little incident with that gust of wind and the reckless boy had proved lucky, hadn't it? And it had to be true because he showed us the squashed hat. Well, yes, except that my schoolfriend was at the gate when the speaker's departing car paused there and he saw the worthy man sitting in the back with an open case in which he was arranging two black hats—one damaged, the other not. We reckoned he was a bit of a con artist—and our respect for him rose accordingly.

Openers

Here's a whole bunch of opening lines that have proved their worth over the years. Don't expect to like them all. They are not really intended to make you laugh as you see them in print. It's how and where you use them that makes them valuable to you. And, as I've illustrated, whatever is intrinsically comical in these openers will remain funny in many different contexts.

All-purpose

"Thanks. At this moment I am trying to remember the ABC of public speaking. ABC. Always Be Confident. And before standing up to face an audience, I also try to remember the XYZ of public speaking. XYZ. Examine Your Zipper."

"May I begin by thanking you for the three great human qualities—faith, hope and charity. Your applause before I speak, that's faith. Applause during my speech—that's hope. Applause after I've spoken, that'll be charity."

"I make a lot of speeches and they can't all be different, I'm afraid. Inevitably I repeat myself. Much of what I'm about to say to you now I used in a speech only recently. So I do apologize to any of you who have heard it before."

"Thank you for that introduction and applause. You're just like my first wife—you build me up for one minute, then make me do all the work for the next half-hour."

"Thank you, I appreciate your welcome because I just felt slightly unwell. I told your very sympathetic Chairman that I was feeling funny and he said, 'Well, do your speech before it wears off.'"

81

"Forgive me if I appear a little shaken but on the way here I was involved in one of the greatest train robberies of all time. I had an Amtrack breakfast."

If you are late

"Sorry I was late arriving but I've been at a meeting of the Procrastinators Society. They've elected me Past President."

"Sorry I was late but there are eight people living in our house and the alarm was only set for seven."

"Sorry I was late but I had a blow-out on the Freeway. Serves me right for eating that spicy dinner."

"Sorry I was late but I had to accept an urgent phone call from a woman I once used to go out with. My wife."

To a large audience

"Thank you. I'm not crazy about making speeches but I've been married for 35 years and this is the only chance I get to see if my mouth still works."

"The Chairman has just said to me, 'Would you like to begin your speech now . . . or shall we let them go on enjoying themselves a little longer?'"

"May I begin by thanking the Banquet Manager for tonight's magnificent dinner which will always have a special place in my heartburn."

"I have asked if I might speak to you before (name of next speaker) makes his speech because I have several engagements in (name the month after next) that I really must keep."

"Tonight I am appearing free of charge and I think you'll agree I'm worth every penny of it."

After a leg-pulling introduction

"Let me thank you for that *kind* introduction. I won't say what kind."

"Thank you. And may I say of all the many introductions I've had over the years that was the most (pause) . . . recent."

After a flattering introduction

"After hearing such a wonderful description the only person who'd expect *me* to stand up would be my mother."

"Wife swapping, getting duty-free booze delivered to your home, sex secrets of the First Family, ways to cut your income tax in half, and How To Get An Audience's Attention So You Can Talk To Them About (your subject). And now that I've got it . . ."

At an expensive function

"What a lavish occasion! The head of the IRS couldn't afford to attend this function. But he's got a man round the front of the building taking the names of everyone who could."

"I warned the Chairman that I wouldn't have time to prepare a speech and he told me just to say something off the top of my head, so—here's a short talk on dandruff."

"It's a privilege to rise to my feet here today and speak before some of the greatest crowned teeth of Europe."

After a confusing speaker

"Well, they do say it's tough to follow one of (name)'s speeches and that's certainly true tonight. I couldn't follow a damned word of it."

After a long speech

"What a mesmerizing speech . . . I enjoyed every month of it."

"What an amazing speech that was. Although I was sad to see that during the course of that speech, several people left the room (pause) . . . married and had children."

If the audience includes a well-known fast driver

"May I say it's a great pleasure to be here. Now a lot of speakers begin their speeches by saying that and they don't mean it. But I really mean it, it's a pleasure. Because I was given a lift here by (name) and the way he drives, it's a pleasure to get anywhere."

If you follow soon after the toastmaster

"Thank you. While waiting to speak I've been fascinated to watch how many people present were longing for that toast in order to light up. Only last Sunday our minister was telling the local flock, 'It all starts with that first cigarette. That first cigarette leads to the first glass of whisky . . . which in turn leads to the first immoral woman!' And a voice from the back of the church yelled, 'And where can we buy these terrific cigarettes?'"

"Thank you for your hospitality and a magnificent luncheon. The Banquet Manager just told me the good news about radio-active lamb. Apparently it kills off most of the salmonella in the kebabs."

If you drop your notes as you rise

"I haven't started talking yet and my speech has already fallen flat."

Truth is Funnier than Fiction

When you read a politician's biography of the news reports of political debates, look out for humorous incidents and note them down. Many are far funnier than anything found in a joke book, mainly because they are not artificial contrivances but actually happened. One British statesman had a fund of such tales in his collection and wove them sparingly but brilliantly into his speeches, using the facts but improving their shape to create a funnier effect. He recalled Churchill in his declining years as a giant of undiminished wit. Two new young MPs in the back benches watched the old man as he dozed on the Front Bench during a recess. One whispered, "I hear he's almost blind now." The other muttered, "And I'm told he's nearly senile." Churchill's voice rumbled out loud and clear: "And they do say the poor old sod's deaf as well."

Convertibles

The Churchill riposte probably works best when it is attributed to him. But many other anecdotes can easily be switched from the original source to fit a new context. Take this closing paragraph which Lyndon B. Johnson often used when he was president.

"I think it essential that the USA remain a two-party country, although I've a weakness for small parties too. And the Republican Party can't be too small to suit me."

Too American to switch elsewhere? Not really. LBJ had already switched it. Disraeli made the same joke about the Liberal Party over a hundred and twenty years ago.

Here's another example. The Russian comedian Yakov Smirnoff told me this story about three Muscovites discussing the precise meaning of fame. The first says. "Fame is being invited to the Kremlin for a chat with President Gorbachev." The second disagrees. "No, fame is being invited to the Kremlin for a chat with Premier Gorbachev and the hot line rings and, rather than interrupt his conversation with you *he ignores it!*" Then the third man speaks up. He says, "You're both wrong. Fame is being invited to the Kremlin for a chat with Premier Gorbachev and the hot line rings, Gorbachev answers it, then holds out the phone and says, 'Here, *it's for you!*'" It's a sound story and will work just as well when applied to Number Ten Downing Street or the White House.

Then there's that apocryphal account of Lady Astor saying to Churchill, "If you were my husband, Winston, I would poison your brandy." Churchill replies, "If you were my wife, Nancy, I would drink it." Wouldn't that fit Anne Edwards and George Bush?

Many smart political exchanges suit application to the commercial world. "The boss of Coca Cola was told that one of his most ruthless executives had his eye upon the presidential chair. He said, 'Maybe, but look what I've got on it.'" This yarn will serve to demonstrate the quick wit of any of today's movers and shakers. It was told in the Thirties about FDR and his challenger Wendell Wilkie. Who knows to what earlier cast of antagonists it may have been attributed?

GIVING THEM WHAT THEY LIKE

Matching your choice of anecdotes to the nature of the audience is easy when the group is specialized—medical jokes for doctors, religious jokes for clergy, golfing jokes for golfers and so on. You'll find some reliable gags for such occasions listed in the chapter "In and Out of Humorous Classics". All are tried and tested.

If the crowd is all-male from various walks of life, you're safe with sports stories. An audience composed of housewives will respond well to humorous tales about lazy husbands, the funny things children say, the nightmare of driving and shopping on a Friday evening and other subjects that concern them regularly. If there are high-profile characters present who are familiar to all, your selection of stories can be based on what they do for a living or for fun, the cars they drive, even the football teams they support.

Help Them to Feel Like a Special Group

You can flatter an audience without them realizing it, just by acknowledging their status. It shows that you have a real comprehension of their specialized world. I had to give a speech for 300 married couples in the retail grocery business. Everyone present ran a neighborhood shop. Here's my opening:

"You do look well. It's reassuring to look around me and see how healthy six hundred people can be despite living off a diet made up exclusively from food that's passed its sell-by date."

The laughter was magic but there was nothing magical about the thought process behind the line or the service it performed. All I had done was take the time to think about the life of a neighborhood grocer. As the various aspects of the trade occurred to me I jotted down headings: Going to the Wholesalers, Limited space for Display Ads, Having to carry new lines advertised on TV, Lines that don't sell, Hours when you can't sell booze, Borrowing from the till, Dated food—ahah! Surely customers won't buy food that has passed its sell-by date and yet it seems unlikely that the small grocer could afford to dump it. Then I knew I had my opening line. Rather than *accuse* them of consuming food that might be on the turn I turned it into a compliment—"You do look well"—before revealing my knowledge of their secret, a fact which most of them would have supposed to be their own personal little habit. By their concerted laughter they discovered that everyone around them ate out-dated food too. They were a special group.

86

Something Unique Irritates Them—Use It

In every trade new irritations arise each year, There's almost certain to be some source of annoyance peculiar to your audience, and it's just sitting there waiting for you to exploit it. It may be a business competitor who's undercutting them, a fault in their supply service, shortage of office space, a surfeit of paperwork, unsociable working hours, overseas bosses, an overmanned boardroom—ahah!

"Your hardworked management team has a well-deserved reputation for dedication and hard work so you can hardly blame them if they occasionally relax and play a little game. In fact, they've devised their very own boardroom version of Musical Chairs. It differs from the usual version in one respect—every time the music stops, they *add* a chair."

Are they resentful of a lazy department?

"I must say I admire the honesty of your Public Relations Director. I asked him how many people worked in his department and he said, 'About half.'"

Does the Sales Force feel aggrieved about slow deliveries?

"And I'd like to add a personal tribute to Wally Walters and his admirable department which, he tells me, is not at all behind schedule. By the way, next Friday is his office Christmas Party."

It's nearly always there if you dig for it. Prying for such information may be irksome but it pays dividends when you speak.

Your Very Best Target Is In Your Mirror

Nearly all the good humorous speakers I've talked to have suggested the same thing—before you mock anything else, mock yourself. Let them see you're a good sport. Let them also see that you can afford to knock yourself—it's a subtle demonstration of your underlying confidence. It offends nobody. What's more, if you are seen to be able to take it, it follows that you are allowed to dish it out. Self-mockery somehow grants you license to have a pop at others. A favorite speaker at many functions is also my insurance agent. He's an expert at disarming his listeners by spiking his own guns first.

"I stand before you, a man who has done for insurance what King Herod did for Toys R Us."

HOW TO BE POSITIVELY INSULTING

It goes under many titles: sarcasm, witty abuse, satire, fun-poking, ridicule, derision, irony, joshing, teasing, good-natured chaffing. The idea of kidding someone is at the heart of classic comedy. Laughing at the boss, at the rich and famous, at the beautiful and strong, that's key comedy for any speaker.

Of course, comedians do it and you're not a comedian. But that doesn't disqualify the use of clever insult humor in your speech. Without seeming to aspire to a new career as the second Groucho, you can win the crowd's approval, improve their mood and increase your control of their attitude by exploiting this simple truth: people like to laugh at other people and they like the person who helps them to do that.

On Your Mark

Let's try an insult. The target: Wally Walters. What do we know about Wally? First, most of the people in the audience know Wally pretty well. Second, Wally thinks he's a VIP. Third, Wally's well known to be a Roman Catholic but isn't self-conscious about his faith. Okay, we're ready for Mr. Walters:

"It's a pleasure to see Wally Walters here tonight and to share the good news that Wally has at last managed to arrange an audience with the Pope."

The crowd is smiling. You've picked on someone they know and can see and you've made a mildly impudent reference to his religion. Now for the twist:

"Up until now, Wally hasn't been able to spare the time."

Pop! You've pricked the balloon you inflated with the straight line. It's a comedy trick that works every time—set-up line and punchline. In the set-up you attracted the audience's attention to your target. You included a familiar fact about Wally to show that you know him as well as anyone else present but you didn't just say, "Wally's a Roman Catholic." You made the reference to his religion obliquely and with humorous exaggeration. No-one really believes Wally's got an actual appointment with His Holiness so the fiction is mildly funny to this crowd. In fact, they don't even know that you've got a punchline coming, your set-up line about Wally seems to be complete on its own. Then comes the topper, a simple reversal of Wally's relationship to a busy religious leader; the little man is more important than the great man. Wally's well-known self-importance is your real angle and the funniest aspect of his reputation.

You'll encounter some audiences so eager to laugh at Wally's ego that your joke doesn't need the deception of a set-up line:

"Nice of Wally Walters to spare us a bit of time between hearing confessions."

Either way, Wally has to be a popular choice of target. You have to know that the audience will enjoy your having fun at his expense and that they won't mind your reference to Wally's faith. Now suppose that your instinct tells you that Wally's vanity is an acceptable angle for you to use, but his Catholicism is not. Then what else is widely known about him? Nothing? Okay then, let's make something up about him, something innocuous that doesn't matter:

"I've known Wally Walters for quite a while and yet I never knew until today that Wally is ambidextrous, which must be very handy for him. He can pat himself on the back with either hand."

Or, if Wally's delusions of grandeur of himself are enough on their own:

"Wally has a very tastefully appointed office. Nothing fancy—just a full-length mirror and a throne."

Keep It Friendly

Obviously, ribbing a recognized personality in such a way must be seen to be good-natured. If everyone in the room knows that Wally has just been promoted over your head, I'm sure you'll agree that he probably ceases to be a legitimate target for your leg-pulling. But in the atmosphere of goodwill normal on most occasions where a speech is given, a little witty sniping at the best-known characters present will always score highly. And the more highly placed his target, the louder the laugh.

Political Potshots

Quite often we begin to sense genuine feeling behind insult jokes when politicians become the target. Everyone is entitled to a political attitude and a jibe at anyone currently active in that arena takes on an extra cutting edge. There's some real bite in President John F. Kennedy's classic comment: "You can always tell when Richard Nixon is lying. His lips move."

Here the bite owes much of its power to the fact that a real life politician is talking about his real-life opponent/enemy. Nevertheless, the same line can be levelled at almost any politician today, and not necessarily by another politician, and score with an audience which shares that view of the person's duplicity. Even if they don't, they may well laugh if the joke has a good angle; people like to laugh at authority in all its forms.

The excitement within the laughter evoked by political sarcasm is tapped by our daily involvement with today's world administrators and the leaders who oppose them, those who are powerful or wish to become powerful. We often find them rather frightening or ridiculous and so perfect fodder for laughs.

THINGS TO AVOID

Many novices see it as a speaker's privilege to tease an audience. I heard one address a Women's Institute and try to make them laugh at feminine weaknesses instead of masculine. It was exactly the same uphill task as trying to make a crowd of electrical retailers laugh at electrical retailers instead of at their customers and suppliers. Yes, it's possible to get an audience to laugh at itself but it isn't easy. In the words of the great Sammy Cahn, "Being good is hard enough—why make it harder?"

Don't Bite The Hand That Claps You

Worse still is when a speaker thinks his audience is a legitimate target for outright rudeness. I have seen it happen with speakers and with comedians, usually the inexperienced variety. Their jokes misfire and they react by attacking the very people they should be stroking. It requires a personality of exceptional warmth and popularity to amuse his audience with lines like:

"Could you sit up in your seats, please? These jokes are going over your heads."

"Sure you people don't have to be up early for the harvest?"

"I think I'll go down to Hertz and rent a faster audience."

And so on. Lines like these are called "joke savers" in show business. They can also be "speech sinkers"; avoid them.

Don't Make Jokes In The Open Air

If the affair is al fresco, dump the humor. Nothing is funny in a field. This mob waiting for you to open a fete, judge a donkey derby, or crown a beauty queen is not an audience in the normal meaning of the word. Out-of-doors is death to comedy. The speaker system will echo or stutter, so anything you say must be slow and clear and declamatory. That sort of delivery kills jokes and, even if it doesn't, you can't hear the laughter. It's gone with the wind.

Beware Repeating Other Speakers' Material

The rule here is: never repeat the joke subject of a previous speaker unless you have a topper. I was told by a businessman of a joke which never failed to win him a good laugh when he spoke at commercial functions. He'd applied the gag to various well- endowed female stars over the years—Jane Russell, Liz Taylor, Raquel Welch, Dolly Parton, all had featured in the joke at some time or other. Now he'd decided to bring it up to date by using actress Brigette Nilssen. His line was, "Running your own business—it's like Brigette Nilssen doing handstands—the overheads can smother you."

That evening he was waiting to be introduced by the Chairman who talked briefly about claims for tax deductions and joked, "I'm told even Brigette Nilssen has deducted $2,000 for her bras—she listed them as 'upkeep'." The little quip scored a little laugh and my friend decided that it need not pre-empt his own joke. He was wrong. If he'd reverted to Dolly Parton's upholstery the laugh would have been saved, but his second use of Miss Nilssen's name killed the joke.

In my experience it is a puzzling but invariable rule that an audience will only find a subject funny once per evening. The speaker using the subject for the first time that night may play with it and perhaps develop it into a vehicle for several one-liners, but when he's finished with it, it's finished for you too. It's the reason why a top-of-the-bill comedian likes to hear which subjects have been mentioned by the comics who have been on before him, instantly dropping any gags on the same topic.

The only exception to this law is the use of a topper to the joke that's been done earlier. It has to be a memorable joke, maybe a story that uses an oft-repeated phrase. Then, if the subsequent speaker can find a way to weave that phrase into his own speech, he can collect appreciation for his spontaneous invention.

The Topical Topper

I remember a toast to the guests in which the speaker told a story about an indiscreet fool, over-sexed and over sixty, who meets a callgirl called Fifi, and in the narrative of the joke, rips his trousers and has to remove them. Fifi was mentioned a number of times and the story ended with the fool being caught by his wife. In the reply to the toast the guest speaker gave his usual amusing speech in which he read out various fictitious apologies from famous people who couldn't attend. As he reached the final scrap of paper, he frowned at the scribbled message and said to the previous speaker, "Oh, and I think this is for you, Frank. Fifi just phoned and your trousers are mended if you want to pick them up."

That was a topper worth using and the room responded with the sort of happy laughter reserved for an opportunity well seized. Toppers can only work if they arise naturally from something that's well established in the minds of the audience, whether it's a good joke, a bad joke, a widely recognized mistake, or some other event which clearly invites further comment.

By the way, please don't let me leave you with the impression that you cannot profitably repeat an "old" joke. Someone once said, "There's no such thing as an old joke, only one they've heard

before." A sure-fire gag is treasure and will stand regular repetition for decades. No, the only "old joke" to avoid is one that's
been used by a previous speaker.

My Favorite
After-Dinner Crackers

Recently an Editor on *The Sun* phoned me after I had been presented with the After-Dinner Speaker of the Year Award by the President of the Guild of Professional Toastmasters, and naturally I was called upon to "say a few words." Reporters and photographers recorded the occasion for the press, articles and pictures duly appeared and as usual, three or four of my wittier lines were reported. The Sun Editor wanted more.

"Send me your twenty best after-dinner lines," he said. "There'll be a cheque for $1,000 sent to the Stars Organization for Spastics if I get them by tomorrow afternoon."

He got them first thing in the morning. In fact, I sent him thirty of my smartest all-purpose speech gags so that he could pick out the twenty that suited *Sun* readers best. I figured he could omit the ten subtle ones.

I would like to have sent him some great lines I've heard from other speakers over the years but he was after my stuff. Pity. I could have included a marvelous line from a speech made for the Food and Drink Federation by the Secretary of Agriculture. He rose to propose the Toast to the Federation, surveyed the room with interest and said:

"This is the first time I've spoken in this room . . . except during other people's speeches."

I could have mentioned this introduction to a rival wit:

"Our next speaker is one you'll remember for the rest of your life. If you have a phenomenal memory. And absolutely nothing else to think about. And you meet with a fatal accident on your way home."

Or this introduction from a Texan comedy writer, who squinted at the page in his hand and said:

"It's my privilege and pleasure to introduce a public speaker of the highest magnitude, a man whose wit is legendary, who is sought after by every organization, who honors us by his presence here tonight . . . and who writes his own introductions."

Or the opening George Burns used when he rose to address the famous Friars Club in New York. His lifelong friend Jack Benny was also being honored that evening and had lost the toss to decide which of them should speak first.

"I want to thank the Friars for giving Jack and myself this beautiful dinner and it's a good thing you didn't wait much longer. At our age, every time we sit down to eat it could be the Last Supper."

And he ended a typically great Burns speech by saying:

"In conclusion I want to thank the Friars for honoring me tonight. But before I sit down I must tell you I thought of a very, very funny closing line. It's hilarious—but I just found out that Jack Benny thought of the same line. And since, as I've said, we've been friends for fifty-five years and to show you what a nice man I am, I'm going to let Jack do that line and I'm going to sit down without getting a laugh."

When a function was held in a particularly shabby hotel, one speaker said:

"Far be it from me to criticize my accommodation but you know there's something lacking in a hotel when you notice that the Gideon Bibles are in paperback."

In reply to some jocular ribbing from a rather aggressive Advertising Director, I recall hearing a Production Manager respond:

"Contrary to popular belief, Fred's mother and father *were* married. Not to each other, no, but they *were* married."

Former President Ronald Reagan has always been a master of comic delivery, knowing the value of self-deprecation. He told a mainly Hollywood audience:

"When I say something, people know I'm not lying—I was never that good an actor."

Campaigning for election Reagan reminded his listeners that the Roman emperor Diocletian had tried price controls and they hadn't worked. Then he added, "And I'm the only one here old enough to remember that."

It was airline chief Freddie Laker who kidded his staff:

"If you have any further ideas about how to rescue this company, please drop them in the suggestion box down the hall. And don't forget to flush it."

So much for quoting others, now I'll quote me. Bearing in mind all that has been said about the correct placement of comedy in a speech and the suitability of the comic dart to the perfect bullseye, here are the thirty crackers I "sold" to *The Sun*. Apply them shrewdly to the right occasion and the right people and you'll score.

1. "Ladies and Gentlemen . . . Mr. Chairman, I really enjoyed your little talk. It was up to your usual substandard.
2. Thank you for that speech. Linguists tell us there are 35,000 useless words in the English language and you hit every damn one of them tonight.
3. And so we come to the speeches. The speeches give everyone who didn't get indigestion from the meal a second chance.
4. Preparing for a speech is like preparing for a big football match. You eat correctly, get plenty of rest and abstain from sex. And I promise you that I have eaten correctly, have had plenty of rest, and will abstain from sex during this speech. (Immediately afterwards, watch out!)

5. We all know the boss is a strict man. He once received a ransom note for his children and sent it back to the kidnappers for re-typing.

6. But in your defense, Sir, we know that we haven't seen all of your management skills and techniques. Company policy expressly forbids beatings.

7. Aggressive? This morning, the receptionist said, 'Have a nice day,' and he said, 'Don't tell me what to do!'

8. What a fine dinner tonight! And everybody's trying to lose weight, I even know a cannibal who's on a diet—he only eats midgets.

9. You know what we can all expect tomorrow, don't you? A Champagne Hangover: the wrath of grapes!

10. The Company Secretary doesn't like to drink—it's just something to do while he gets drunk.

11. Our Advertising Director can take credit for a lot of things, but he's always willing to share a little with the person who actually did it.

12. What can I say about our Sales Director? He's been called cold, rude, self-centered, arrogant and egotistical. But that's just his family's opinion.

13. Our Marketing Manager is a man with a conscience. He's not an ordinary drunk. He donated his body to science and he's preserving it in alcohol until they use it.

14. Let me salute our Financial Director, a man so thrifty, he found a box of corn plasters, so he went out and bought a pair of tight shoes.

15. George is spruced up for this occasion. Even went to the barber. After the new barber gave him a really close shave, he asked for a glass of water. 'Are you feeling faint?' asked the barber. George said, 'No, I just wanted to see if my face is leaking.'

16. Among us tonight are politicians and doctors. Doctors are like politicians: they view with alarm so they can point with pride.

17. We have some younger folk present and I admire the youth of today. I saw these kids carrying a sign: 'MAKE LOVE NOT WAR!' I'm married—I do both.

18. I greet the insurance experts here tonight. They know that there are two kinds of liars in car accidents. Both drivers.

19. The ladies look lovely but they don't know everything. Ask any woman her age and nine times out of ten she'll guess wrong.

20. Take Joan Collins. She even lies about her dog's age.

21. Maybe it's true that *life* begins at 40. But everything else starts to wear out, fall out or spread out.

22. Don't worry about avoiding temptations as you grow older. They will avoid you first.

23. Today in 1989 we're having a retail sales boom. It's weird to go shopping! You would never believe how many different things a bargain hunter would rather have than money.

24. And how about today's morals? The big question is: Can a girl be a good girl if she returns home from a date with a Gideon Bible under her arm?

25. I just hired a detective to watch my wife—not that she's unfaithful. I just want to know where she is when I am.

26. Is my shirt behaving? I always have trouble with laundries. The last one I sent my shirts to lost the buttonholes.

27. We have legal experts here tonight and I respect you all. My lawyer helped me lose 125 pounds of fat—he got me a divorce.

28. We have medical experts here and I respect you too. My doctor's very shrewd. He kept me in his waiting room so long I caught four other diseases.

29. Two chaps talking at a bar. One said, 'I got married because I was tired of going to the laundromat, eating junk food and wearing socks with holes in them.' The other fellow said, 'That's funny: I got divorced for the same reasons.

30. Finally, a toast to your sex lives: 'May you live as long as you want to . . . and want to as long as you live.

In And Out Of
Humorous Classics

Doctor Freud says there's no such thing as a new joke. No, nor a new plot, a new tune, a new design or a new day. Everything new is derivative to a certain extent, Herr Doctor, I understand that. But I've spent the past 45 years or so making up jokes by shuffling familiar words and ideas into a novel order. In the course of this rather absurd but lucrative career, millions of sentences have been produced which, when spoken out loud, make people laugh. These could reasonably be regarded as new jokes because no one has thought of them or said them before. But after they've been heard, then what are they?

Well, the weak ones are scrap paper. The moderately funny ones go into the file for twisting, polishing and possible further employment. And the really good ones become old friends. There is nothing wrong with using an old joke. On the contrary, if it's funny and appropriate, there is everything right with using it. You just need to grace it with the proper setting.

Once you have got a few well-chosen yarns in your repertoire and they've gone down well a few times, there's no need to abandon them for the sake of change. Provided the audience is different, you can find security in repeating stories in which you have confidence in all sorts of contrasting situations. Just ease your way into them with words that seem to apply only to the particular place, time and people.

The old friend is a reliable laugh-getter that both you and most other people can still enjoy. You may have heard a comedian tell a comic tale that's immediately familiar to you and thought, "I like this story." Then you've heard the happy laughter from his audience and perhaps you've wondered how much of it was surprise and how much recognition, pleasant recognition of an old friend. For the speaker, such old friends are just as trustworthy—but you've got to treat them well and introduce them properly.

Public radio provides the right language for this sort of thing. Old radio shows aren't old, they're "listeners' requests from the Golden Age of Broadcasting." The umpteenth showing of some TV warhorse isn't a repeat, it's "another chance to see the vintage Award-winner." Re-runs at Christmas and Easter are "traditional fare" and if the star died last week it's "a special tribute." Our old friend only needs the same treatment—introduce it as "a classic."

With one word—"classic"—you simultaneously disarm critics and set a seal of semi-immortality on the yarn you're about to spin. You're not claiming it's new. On the contrary, you're proclaiming its status as a Golden Oldie. No one can jeer at the age of an antique, can they?

The way a speaker flows naturally from his speech into an anecdote takes a little thought, but it's so worthwhile in its effect. How often have you winced at a clumsy transition or a hoary cliché: "Which reminds me of the story of . . ."

I heard a speaker interrupt himself in just this way with a quite unsuitable joke and it's stayed in my mind ever since. Here was this physicist giving us some simple and enthralling stuff about the miniature universe of the atom, when he decided we needed a laugh. His narrative switched as if he'd changed TV channels and he was off into a story about a teacher lecturing on sex morality. The punchline got a titter because it was, and still is, a good little joke. And then he jerked us back into his sub-atomic world so fast we all suffered tiny hernias in our attention. Wrong story for the moment, wrong way in and out of it.

Use the examples below to suit circumstances which are appropriate to you, your speech, the setting and the audience. If you plan to keep a card-file, put these in for starters. The format is, I hope, self-explanatory. I have suggested an "In," followed by a suitable story, followed in most instances by an "Out" which sets you back on course for the rest of your speech. Where there is no "Out," I have assumed you can safely be left to carry on by yourself.

FOLLOWING A BRILLIANT INTRODUCTION "For that magnificent introduction, I thank you . . . I think. It was so good, I can hardly wait to hear what I'm going to say. I just hope I can live up to it.

"These are what are known as 'mixed feelings', a term once defined as watching your mother-in-law drive over a cliff in your new car. There's another classic example that comes to mind but this one is true. Shortly after the death of Noel Coward, Peter Ustinov was preparing a TV program in tribute to his memory and his music. A rather arrogant young composer buttonholed Ustinov with an elegy he had composed in honor of Coward and he insisted on playing it to him at once. Tolerantly Ustinov postponed his next appointment and listened to the twenty-minute piece until the last note had died away. 'Well?' demanded the composer. 'What do you think?' 'I think,' said Ustinov, 'that it would have been better if you had died and Noel Coward had written the elegy.'

"Dear Sir, I think it might have been better if you were making this speech and I had made the introduction . . ."

THIS BEAUTIFUL CITY "Your city is blessed with its magnificent cathedral, historic churches, many fine libraries and parks and a widely envied museum. The museum staff is especially helpful to ignorant visitors like me.

"I asked an attendant, 'How old is that Roman pottery?' and he said 'Seventeen hundred years, five weeks and two days.' I said, 'How can you pinpoint its date with such astonishing accuracy?'

And he said. 'No problem, sir. It was seventeen hundred years old when I took this job and I've been here exactly five weeks and two days.'

"But my inquiries about this function have provided much more reliable information . . ."

THE USE OF LANGUAGE "Some people use language to express thought, some to conceal thought. Far too many of us use it to replace thought. Mark Twain had his own views on languages. He said that a gifted person ought to learn English in thirty hours, French in thirty days and German in thirty years. But is the English tongue really so simple?

"Only last week I noticed an odd quirk in our language, When we talk about an East Wind or a West Wind, we mean the direction the wind's coming from. But when we say clockwise or counter-clockwise, we mean the direction the clock's going to. And that, I suppose, explains why we run out of wind before we run out of time.

"If I'm not careful, I may be in danger of doing the opposite—running out of time before I run out of wind . . ."

BEING CLEARLY UNDERSTOOD "Naturally, we all want to be understood. Equally, naturally, and important, none of us wants to be misunderstood. To that end, we should employ language not only to express our ideas but also to convey them comprehensibly to others.

"The IBM scientists have been working for years now on the perfect translator, a computer which could turn the United Nations Building from a Tower of Babel into Harmony Hall. Their acid test of an ideal machine is that when it has translated a phrase from the first language to the second, it should be able to translate the same phrase from the second language back to the first and come up with the exact original wording. A laudable ambition but one which doesn't account for our English ambigu-ities. Into the computer went our well-known saying, 'Out of sight, out of mind'. It was translated into Russian. Then the Russian version was retranslated to English again. Guess what! 'Out of sight, out of mind' came back as 'Invisible insanity'.

"Doesn't that accidental phrase describe to a T the workings of certain political minds? ..."

TOUGH PROBLEMS, SIMPLE SOLUTIONS "Even the most experienced panel of experts can miss the answer to a professional dilemma precisely because they are experienced. They are able to identify all the complex difficulties obstructing their normal procedure—but a fresh and unpracticed eye may be more alert to the existence of another approach altogether.

"*Remember the classic tale of the truck that got stuck under a bridge and a crowd gathers and no-one knows what to do? Some say tear the top off the truck, others say dismantle the bridge. The argument rages—top off the lorry, dismantle the bridge. Finally a small child at the back asks, 'Why don't you let the air out of the tires?'*

"We should always be open to a new approach to our problems from someone with an uncluttered viewpoint. They may let the air out of our tires before an opponent takes the wind out of our sails ..."

AGE AND ADVANTAGES As one grows older, Nature compensates a little bit for one's diminishing powers in curious ways. Some old folks increase in their philosophical understanding and feeling for human nature.

"*My great-uncle's a wonderful octogenarian living in an Old Folk's Home. There's a little old lady in there who's got her eye on him, and she claims to have gypsy blood. She told me, 'I feel so close to your great-uncle. Why, I can even tell where he's from and how old he is.' I said, 'How?' and she slid her hand under his bedsheet, groped about a bit and said, 'You're a Capricorn, still very vigorous, married three times, 81 years old and born in Ohio!' He said, 'You're right! How can you tell all that?' She said, 'You told me yesterday.'*

"Growing old isn't so bad when you consider the alternative ..."

CUSTOMS AND MOTIVES "When first encountering any human mystery or arcane custom, look first for the simplest motive. People have acted according to the same basic reasoning since history began.

I was travelling in the Atlas Mountains of Morocco, a part of the world steeped in tradition and superstition, when I saw an Arab riding a donkey while his wife walked fifteen paces behind him. I said, 'Excuse me, but why are you riding the donkey while your wife is walking?' and he said, 'She hasn't got a donkey.' A few weeks later I was in Lebanon and I saw another Arab riding a donkey while his wife walked fifteen paces in front of him. Again I asked why and he said, 'Landmines.'

"Obviously, Women's Lib has yet to make its mark in the Middle East, whereas here tonight the ladies have it firmly established . . ."

PROSPECTS AND RESPONSIBILITY "Are we ready to accept the responsibilities of future success? Well, whenever I'm asked if I can handle a situation, I tend to examine the thinking behind the question.

"Unlike the suitor courting a lovely girl, whose father interviews him. 'Do you think you're earning enough to support a family?' says he. 'I certainly do,' says the boy. 'Think carefully now,' says his future father-in-law. 'There's twelve of us.'

"But we face challenges more cautiously examined and found to be "acceptable . . ."

PUZZLING SITUATIONS "Of course it's frustrating to find yourself in a predicament where, no matter how much thought you bring to bear, the solution simply refuses to dawn through the fog."

"As in the classic story of the guy walking home from a bar when a real pea-souper comes down. Luckily he's got his walking stick so he taps his way along. Suddenly there's nothing there in front of him. Must be the end of a pier or the rim of a cliff! So he feels around behind him—nothing! The only thing to do is stand very still until the fog lifts in the morning . . . and when it does, there he is, standing in the middle of the street with the end broken off his stick.

"The solution we need to any puzzle may be hidden by just such a fog that only needs our imagination to disperse it . . . ."

IS THE CUSTOMER ALWAYS RIGHT? "Keeping the customer satisfied is sound company credo. Can it be carried too far? Has a company ever gone bankrupt by allowing its customers to dictate the style of service, variety of product or its trading policy? Well, the line has to be drawn somewhere this side of running a charity.

"The Chief Executive of Italy's biggest supermarket chain told me a story about a rather unimaginative thief who plans to rob one of their suburban stores. He needs an excuse to go up into the manager's office so he thinks, 'I'll complain about the choice of goods.' He walks in and there's the manager on his knees putting the day's takings in the safe. 'I want to complain.' 'Yes, sir, what's your complaint?' 'You've got no coffins.' 'Coffins? In a supermarket? Are you mad? Go to the funeral parlor. We don't sell coffins!' The manager turns away to close the safe and the thief seizes his chance, pulls out a club and cracks him over the head—THWACK! And the manager says, 'Okay, okay! I'll get some in tomorrow!'

"Italy also gave us the Latin motto which is implicit in all customer-related trading—*Caveat emptor,* let the buyer beware. I would add let the vendor beware too. When you cut back on your prices, you may have to cut back on your quality and so eventually on the number of customers. A bargain takes two and both should benefit . . ."

REFUSING AN INVITATION "In accepting your invitation to attend this function, I expressed my gratitude. Had I been unable to accept, I should have expressed my regret, but when we decline an invitation just because we don't want to go, how hypocritically sorry should we pretend to be?"

"George Bernard Shaw was in no two minds about it. An aristocrat seeking his acquaintance sent him an invitation: 'Lady Proctor will be at home on Tuesday, August the Tenth, between four and six in the afternoon.' Shaw returned the invitation. Underneath he had written: 'Mr. George Bernard Shaw likewise.'

"All very well for GBS, but I believe the cause of diplomacy would suffer without its kindly little lies. Shaw, on the other hand, could never resist giving an honest retort if it had the force of wit.

"The self-admiring dancer Isadora Duncan sent him a passionate invitation to father her next child. 'Think what a child it

would be,' she said, 'with my beauty and your brain.' Shaw replied at once. 'Madam, think what a child it would be if it had your brain and my beauty.'

"Had I both the brains and the beauty, then, I might have been one of those rare and privileged creatures whom Shaw would invite to the opening nights of his plays. And here was the clincher.

"Shaw's new play, The Apple Cart, opened in 1929. To Winston Churchill he sent an invitation with the words, 'I enclose two tickets so that you may bring a friend—if you have one.' Churchill returned the tickets with this reply. 'Regret a previous engagement, but could I have tickets for the second night—if there is one?'

"Speaking for myself, I am more than content to give this single performance. Two nights of this speech and I might have no friends . . ."

FALLIBILITY "We should never be deceived that an individual's achievement of high office and great influence means that all that person's private weaknesses have been conquered, although the responsibility of power often means that personal fallibility must be concealed to preserve the unflawed image expected of a leader.

"There was a brilliant admiral, a hero of World War II, who was known for his rigorous Navy discipline and doing everything by the book. It seemed the man had no weaknesses at all, except for one curious little idiosyncracy. Every morning after breakfast he would retire to his state room, open his strong box and study a piece of paper. For years every man who served under him speculated about what was on that page. Then one day the great admiral was called to the bridge urgently and left his quarters without locking his safe. While he was busily occupied, two of his junior officers dared to slip into his cabin and look at the note that he read every morning. It said, 'STARBOARD ON THE RIGHT, PORT ON THE LEFT'.

"If human greatness weren't founded upon a little weakness, it would be neither so great nor so human . . . ."

ACHIEVING A RESULT "Persuading someone to do what you want them to do can often run you right up against a flat rejection. We'll never get anywhere battering our heads against that sort of brick wall. It's much wiser to pause and consider how to climb over it, walk round it or loosen the mortar bit by bit. There's nearly always another way to get people to react as you wish them to.

"*Ask that legendary farmer in (name of local town/village) whose livestock was upset by the motorists speeding past his property at eighty mph. His lawyer told him it would take time and money to bring his case to the attention of the local government officials and argue for a suitable police notice to be erected at the roadside, and even that would probably be ineffective. The shrewd old farmer came up with his own sign and now drivers crawl by his place as slowly as he could wish. It's a big sign and it says, 'PLEASE PROCEED WITH CARE. NUDIST CAMP CROSSING AHEAD.'*

"I shall approach the subject of what I hope to persuade you to do with equal caution . . ."

OBITUARIES "One way to get your name in the newspapers is to walk across (name of local busy street) reading one. I think it was Brendan Behan, the Irish playwright, who said there's no such thing as bad publicity unless it's an obituary notice. And who was it who marvelled over the obituaries in the press. 'Isn't it wonderful,' he said, 'how people manage to die in alphabetical order?'

"*Here's my favorite obituary ever, clipped from an old issue of the (name of local paper). 'FLINDERS, Frederick John: Accidentally killed last Saturday when a bullet ricocheted while he was endeavouring to shoot a rabbit in his vegetable garden. Surviving are his wife, three children and one rabbit.'*

"It makes you ponder on what you'd like them to say about you . . ."

THE CENTER OF INTEREST "An audience's attention can move away from a speaker for the oddest reasons. The Sales Director may have the boardroom in his spell when the coffee cart lady trundles in and, zip, he's lost his grip. A phone rings, a waiter drops a tray, someone topples a glass of wine, or, worse than these, everyone in the room keeps glancing at the Chief Executive after every pleasantry to see if he thinks it's funny before they dare laugh. Comedians suffer that same problem. One admitted he always sent his musicians offstage while he did his nightly patter routines because their glum faces cast a gloom over the crowd.

"Even his Holiness Pope John Paul II is not exempt from these vagaries in group interest. He was Archbishop and Metropolitan of Cracow when he was created cardinal in 1967. As such he attended many glamorous functions where beautiful and shapely ladies were the natural center of attention. But the 47-year-old cardinal confessed to a friend and diplomat, 'The snag with these grand affairs is that every time a lovely lady is presented to me and curtsies in a low-cut gown, no-one is looking at the lady. Everyone is looking at me to see if I'm looking at the lady.'

"Of course, I have you gentlemen at a disadvantage right now. While you're looking at me, I'm looking at the ladies. . . ."

BIOGRAPHY "Your Chairman asked me to supply a biography and I was happy to oblige. I was just grateful he hadn't asked for a pedigree.

"A social climber I know in (name of local town) has just lost interest in his family tree. He paid a genealogist four hundred dollars to dig up information about his ancestors. Now he's had to give him another hundred bucks to keep him quiet.

"Why pay money to have your family tree traced? Just go into politics and your opponents will do it for you. . . ."

PERSPECTIVE "It's always wise to spare a moment to see the other person's point of view. From their angle, matters may seem entirely different.

"A family of lions, sprawled out under a clump of trees in a safari park, looked up as a car packed with eight staring tourists drove slowly past. And the father lion remarked to his brood, 'Dear oh dear! It's really cruel, the way they keep them caged up like that.'"

RETRACTIONS "If I've done anything I'm sorry for, I am always willing to be forgiven. And I'll always accept an apology if it matches the size of the damage.

"A good friend of mine was the subject of an insulting article in a daily newspaper. A week later he ran into the reporter responsible for the article in the men's room of the Plaza Hotel. As the reporter washed his hands he said, 'You know, I've been thinking

about that article we ran last week and I've decided that it was totally unfair. I apologize.' And my friend said, 'I accept your apology—but next time, why don't you insult me in the men's room and apologize in the paper?'"

FIRST IMPRESSIONS "For every salesman, creating that first impression is crucial. You start by winning the customer's confidence, right? But what comes next? Even the least perceptive customer knows that appearances can be deceptive.

"Unlike the gullible missionary wandering in the African jungle when he comes face to face with a hungry lion. Too late to run, so the missionary sinks to his knees and starts to pray. To his amazement the lion also goes down on his knees and starts to pray. The missionary cries, 'It's a miracle! A moment ago I had given up all hope and now this savage beast joins me in holy prayer!' 'Quiet,' growls the lion. 'I'm saying grace.'

"This is one deal the missionary doesn't want to close. But how should you go about winning over the customer? . . ."

WORTH, NOT COST "It's not the price of a thing that's important, it's the value . . . as in the case of an inexpensive but strategically placed button.

"Charlie Chaplin was already a multi-millionaire on a day in the early Thirties when he was visiting the studio of his friend Pablo Picasso. But Chaplin was raised in the poverty of London's East End and the lessons of childhood never left him. Picasso made a sudden gesture and accidentally spilt some paint on Chaplin's white slacks. He said, 'I'm so sorry, Charles! I'll get some spirit and remove it.' And Chaplin said, 'Please don't! Just leave the paint where it is and sign my trousers.'

"As Thoreau said, 'All good things are cheap, all bad things are dear' . . ."

HIRING AS REQUIRED "I've heard it argued that a resident expert on the payroll will cost less than engaging him as a free-lance for each individual project. From his point of view, that might seem quite fair—the security of a regular salary compared with separate fees which subsidize idle periods. But it doesn't take into account the psychology of the maverick, stifled by such security and at his best in precarious independence.

"A tramp came up to me in (name of local town), obviously an educated man down on his luck. He said, 'Excuse me, sir, I don't like to beg but could you spare a few dollars?' I said, 'Yes, but will you spend it on food, drink or shelter?' He said, 'No, sir, to be frank I shall spend it on the favors of a lady of the night, a pleasure I haven't had for months.' I said, 'If you want a woman, why don't you get married?' And he said, 'What, and have to beg for it every night?'

"A man who doesn't care what people think can generally be found at the top of the ladder or at the bottom . . ."

COMMUNICATION AND COMPREHENSION "No-one enjoys the time wasted trying to decipher the gobbledegook of civil service forms, legal documents, even the instructions for programming a video. But are we never guilty of sending messages couched in terms familiar to ourselves but totally impenetrable to the recipients?

"True story: a pregnant woman ran into the Altoona, Pennsylvania, telegraph office and told the operator that her husband had gone off to Philadelphia to have a banner made for the Church Christmas Bazaar & Pageant, but she had forgotten to

tell him how large the banner should be, or which hymnal words should form the inscription. So she sent her husband the following telegram: 'DEAR ANDREW, UNTO US A SON IS BORN, TWO FEET WIDE AND EIGHT FEET LONG.' Andrew never returned to Altoona.

"Customers sometimes never return if the messages they get from us are mysteriously or thoughtlessly expressed . . ."

CRITICISM "Few of us really enjoy criticism but we can usually appreciate its value to us if it is both constructive and fair. Unfair comment or plain abuse is unacceptable—although it can be very entertaining to those who aren't involved.

"Our local Amateur Dramatic Group got a bit ambitious this year and staged their version of King Lear. *It attracted quite a lot of comment but I think this criticism should give you a pretty good idea of what it was like. It's from our local paper: 'On (date), the (name of local town) Players performed Shakespeare's* King Lear *to a full house. The only real benefit to be derived from this production is that it can at last clear up the question as to whether this play was written by Shakespeare or Bacon. All that has to be done is to open up both their graves and see which one turned over last Friday night.'*

"Please, if you have anything as wittily cruel to say about my performance, let it remain as secret as the grave . . ."

HONESTY "We must be astute in our honesty. Too many people think that those qualities are mutually incompatible, that honesty precludes craftiness. It just isn't so. You can be one hundred per cent honest and still use your wits.

"I heard of a lady in (name of local town) who lost her handbag. Some honest person ran after her and returned it. She said, 'That's funny—when I lost it there was a twenty-dollar bill in it. Now there are four five-dollar bills.' And the chap said, 'Yeah. The last time I found a lady's handbag, she didn't have any change for a reward.'"

TECHNOLOGY "Technology is filling our offices and homes with appliances smarter than we are. And some of us may be awe-struck by the computer whizzkids and their complicated apparatus. But we should never forget that the greater the invention, the simpler the common sense that created it.

"Whenever the great inventor Thomas Edison guided visitors around the displays of novel gadgets that filled his home, someone would always ask, 'With everything here so modern and innovative, why do your visitors still have to push their way in through that old-fashioned turnstile?' And Edison would chuckle with delight and say, 'Because, my friend, every single soul who forces his way through that old turnstile pumps three gallons of water up from my well and into my water tank."

PIONEERING "In every business the veteran loves to boast to the novice how tough it was in the early days.

"Best bit of bragging I ever heard was a grizzled old plumber trying to convince his apprentice how hard the job was when he was learning to do it. He said, 'You've got it soft, kid. In the old days they used to let us lay two lengths of piping. Then they'd turn on the water and we had to keep ahead of it!"

THE LESSONS OF EXPERIENCE "Experience is a great teacher. Only trouble is, you get the tests before you learn the lessons.

I know a brilliant young chiropractor who was called in urgently to a Chicago hotel to attend to a highly placed Emir from the Middle East. The Arab aristocrat was in agony until my friend's phenomenal skills at soothing angry vertebrae brought relief. After a week of daily treatment, the Emir was fully restored. The young chiropractor had no idea what fee to charge. He spoke to the Emir's Chicago legal advisor: 'What should I do? Treat him free as an honored visitor or would that be insulting? Should I ask him for one thousand dollars or is that taking advantage of his wealth?' The Emir's legal advisor said, 'Try this—submit your account but leave the amount blank. Simply write across the top of your bill the words "THE EMIR IS ALWAYS FAIR".' Within a month the chiropractor received a check from the Emir for twenty-five thousand dollars! He phoned the lawyer at once to tell him the good news and thank him. Next day the young man received an invoice from the lawyer for his services. The amount had been left blank and across the top of the bill were the words 'THE CHIROPRACTOR IS ALWAYS FAIR'.

"Not too painful a way to learn a lesson about taking professional advice. Perhaps it's time for me to offer you some of mine—at no further cost . . ."

HEAD HUNTING "In every business talent is at a premium. The input of new and gifted recruits can revitalize flagging enthusiasm in factory, office and boardroom. Of course, when you go searching for talent, it all depends what you're looking for.

"I heard of a basketball coach whose favorite fantasy is that a gorgeous, wealthy college student lures him to her dormitory . . . where he meets her brother who is seven foot six."

MEETING A DEADLINE "I once had a boss who liked to give me jobs with precise deadlines and then let me know that he'd given the same task and the same deadline to another of his young aspirants for promotion. He reckoned there was no better spur than setting up a neck-and-neck race between his employees. And it's hard to deny that having the competition breathing down your neck can make you move faster than you ever dreamed you could.

"As in the classic case of the commuter newly moved to the countryside. Desperate to catch his train he called to a farmer busy herding his cows along the road, 'Hey, grandpa! Is it all right with you if I take a shortcut across your field? I've got to catch the 8:15!'

And the farmer said, 'Go ahead, young fella—but if my bull sees you, you'll catch the 7:45.'

"Next time you feel a deadline is beyond your reach, try to imagine that bull is closing in behind you. You'll reach it . . ."

UNTRAINED ASSISTANTS "There are many blessings to becoming an expert but one of the curses that comes with that status is the responsibility for training your apprentices. An assistant who is no assistance at all can be a distinct liability. Should it be part of your job? How else can your experience be passed on?

"The couple next door to me recently had to go to town on business so they told their ten-year-old son to take care of his little sister. He said, 'I'll take her fishing with me, she'll learn something.' When his parents got home his face was dark. 'Never again,' he told his mother, 'I didn't catch a single fish.' She said, 'Never mind, I'm sure she'll learn to be quiet next time.' And the ten-year-old said, 'It wasn't the noise, mom. She ate the bait.'

"When your help is no help, hang on to this thought: there are many times when you can't get help, but there's never a time when you can't give it . . ."

THE CARROT OR THE STICK "These days we no longer expect to be nagged and badgered at work. Instead of being reminded of what failure will bring, we're encouraged by the rewards of success. Domestically though, it doesn't seem to have changed as much. According to a recent survey, 33 per cent of American husbands are henpecked. Do you know how they found out about that? Simple, they just asked the wives for permission to interview the husbands.

"It brings to mind the incredibly henpecked husband who finally did something without his wife's okay—he dropped dead. She was devastated. No-one to moan at, to harass and torment. Her neighbor was sympathetic. She said, 'I can tell you're missing poor Claude.' The widow wiped away a tear and said, 'Oh yes. It seems only yesterday he came up the path, opened that front door, and stood there, letting two flies in.'

"We all know which works better for us—the threat or the promise.

"Remember the king's head torturer who did horrible things to his prisoner to make him admit his guilt in a conspiracy, all without result. Finally, the king tried another tactic. And sure enough, the prisoner confessed. The torturer was astonished. He said, 'Your Majesty, what new agony did you apply?' 'None,' said the king, 'I just offered him something he wanted more than anything in the world.' 'What?' asked the torturer, and the king said, 'To change places with you.'

"It's been said before but it's still true—human beings will never work as hard for rewards as they will for greater ones . . ."

WRONG CONCLUSIONS "At a function I attended a long-winded speaker had been on his feet for forty slow minutes. Then he took a deep breath and embarked on yet another subject, the dangers of hastily formed opinions. He said, 'When I look at your faces I make a judgment about how to speak. I am sure you would not wish me to jump to a conclusion.' A voice from the back rang out, 'Jump to it, run to it, but for pity's sake, get to it soon!' It's all too easy for any speaker to reach a conclusion—both the conclusion of his speech and wrong conclusion about its reception.

"When a Union leader had spoken at some length to a Workers" Co-operative in Shanghai, he sat down to total silence. No-one clapped, no-one cheered, no-one even smiled. Then a Chinese official rose and spoke for about the same duration in Cantonese. This time the audience broke into prolonged cheering. In a generous mood of resignation the leader started to join in the enthusiastic applause. An official from the American Consulate caught his arm and murmured, 'Chill out, sir—it's your speech they're cheering.'

"I hope you won't feel that I need an interpreter to explain my choice of words to you tonight . . ."

REGIONAL SENSIBILITIES "It's dangerously easy to become so immersed in our own affairs that we begin to believe that all the world thinks and moves as we do.

"In Vermont they tell the classic story of a high-powered Boston lawyer who required a deposition from a farming family. He phoned the opposing lawyer and said, 'I'll fly up there next Friday, talk to these farmers and spend the rest of the weekend skiing.' The older lawyer said, 'Next Friday? Oh, no, I don't advise you to come to this part of the world asking questions on next Friday. You would not get much of a welcome.' The Boston lawyer said, 'Welcome? How would they welcome a summons from the judge?' 'Oh boy,' said the older lawyer, 'that would really put their backs up. You see, up here they're mindful of the fact that next weekend is Easter . . . and the last time a person was ordered to be interrogated on a Good Friday, they crucified him.'

"I too must be aware of certain sensibilities here tonight . . ."

COOPERATION AND HOSPITALITY "I thank the organizers for their kind co-operation and my hosts for their hospitality.

"I know a farmer from the Black Country who once explained to me the difference between the two. He said, 'When two cows stand with their heads to each other's tails, flicking the flies off one another's faces, that's cow-operation. And when the same thing happens in the stables, that's horse-pitality.'

"Ah, you're like my father who couldn't stand puns. He said he was contra-puntal . . ."

VANITY "I often think that when success turns a man's head it's a shame it doesn't wring his neck at the same time. But the overblown balloon is all the easier to burst.

"A former Broadway star attempting a comeback was playing in a Pittsburgh theater where he boasted to the manager, 'I'm so popular in New York, they're going to name a new cigar after me.' The blunt manager said, 'Oh, yeah? Well, I hope it draws better than you do.'

"Nevertheless, when praise is due it must be given . . ."

116

POTENTIAL CAPABILITY "Computers, specialized electronics and high-tech systems apart—the truly unlimited capacity for our success lies in only one piece of apparatus, the human brain in the human body.

"They still tell the classic story in Kentucky of a strapping young man brought before the local judge for the possession of a still. He denied using it to make illicit booze. The judge said, 'Come now, George, you can't expect me to believe you haven't been making home brew. Why, the very fact that you own the necessary equipment is proof of your guilt.'George said, 'Then, by God, your Honor, you'd better charge me with sexual assault as well—for though I've never done it, I sure as hell own the necessary equipment!'

"Your future potential depends upon your quality, skill and determination—and, looking around me, I can see you sure as hell own the necessary equipment . . ."

RESEARCH BEFORE JUDGMENT "Naturally I've sought some guidance before taking up your time here today. I checked my facts.

"Even judges seek information from their peers so they can do a better job on the bench. Monica, an elderly lady of the night, stood before the newly appointed Judge Marlowe. She appealed for leniency so pathetically that he had qualms about pronouncing sentence. He called a brief adjournment, then went to the chambers of a senior judge and said, 'Harry, what would you give a sixty-year-old prostitute?' And Harry said, 'About ten bucks.'

"When I asked your Chairman how much he would give a thirty-nine-year-old speaker, he said, 'About twenty minutes.'"

Note: Adjust the age to suit yourself.

RULES AND REGULATIONS "Regulations are meant to do just that—regulate. On the other hand, rules are laid down to help us, not to rule us. Applied over-zealously they can begin to exist purely for their own sake and that's when they cease to help and start to hinder.

"As in the classic case of the rural Colorado couple who decided to celebrate their son's fourth birthday by getting married. They drove their pickup truck into Denver and presented themselves to the proper official. He sent them off to get a license. When

they returned with it, he questioned the bridegroom's name. He said, 'You've put Joe—is your given name Joseph?' 'Yes, sir.' 'Then go back and fill it in correctly.' Back they came with a corrected form whereupon he questioned the bride's name: 'This says Beth—is your given name Elizabeth?' 'Yes, sir.' 'Then go back and fill it in correctly.' When at last they returned with every detail properly filled in, the official scowled at the license and said, 'Well, I have no choice but to marry you but I want to make one thing perfectly clear. That son of yours will still be a technical bastard.' And Joe said, 'That ain't so bad, sir. That's what your clerk said you were.'

"I've been called a lot of things in my time but no one ever said I was technical . . ."

WORKING CONDITIONS "A strong employer deserves a strong Union and vice-versa. If one of them is weak, both can suffer.

"I heard a classic story of one job applicant who said, 'I like the job, sounds fine, but the last place I worked paid more, gave more overtime, more bonuses, subsidies, travel allowances, holidays with pay and generous pension plans.' The potential employer said, 'Why did you leave?' He said, 'The firm went broke.'

"That's the trouble with hard bargains—they can turn out to be hard on everybody . . .'

THANKS TO EVENT COORDINATOR "This has been a marvel of organization and for that we must give our unstinted thanks to the person(s) responsible for it.

"It's been as complicated a piece of administrative juggling as I've seen since my wedding day. I can still hear my bride-to-be saying to her mother, 'Mom, I've still got a million things to take care of and I do want everything to be as perfect as possible. I'm determined not to overlook even the most insignificant little detail.' And her mother replying, 'Don't worry, I'll make sure he's there.'

"Well, tonight's organizer(s) made sure I was here too and I'm very grateful . . ."

SALUTING A CLEVER BUSINESSMAN "Everyone allied in business has benefited from his acumen, either in terms of wealth or experience.

"I first learned to appreciate his application of sound business principles to every kind of occasion when I had the honor of attending his wedding. I remarked to his beautiful bride how I couldn't help but notice that all the guests were married couples. And she said, 'Yes, that's my wonderful husband's idea—isn't it clever? He said if we only invite married people all the presents will be clear profit.'

"In my experience, just having his friendship over the years has been clear profit for me . . ."

PATRIOTISM "Intellectually I know that America is no better than any other country but emotionally I know it is. National pride has less to do with the State than with the state of mind. Of course, patriotism is a little out of style these days, although there are still some areas much admired for the nationalistic zeal of their people.

"I once met a fellow from Duluth, who in his youth saved hard to buy a bicycle and get a job as a delivery boy. With his savings from that he was able to afford the luxury of buying his old mother a train ticket to visit her sister in South Dakota, while he cycled down to keep her company. There she fell ill and, of course, a doctor was sent for. He told the lad that only the pure air of Northern Minnesota could save his mother's life. The boy was equal to the occasion. He carted his bicycle up to his mother's bed, let the air out of the tires—and she lived to be a hundred and two.

"Well, that's what he told me. Maybe it was hot air all the time . . ."

SARCASM "Somebody once said that many a wife sends her husband to an early grave with a series of little digs. But sometimes sarcasm is the last resort of self-respect.

"As in the classic tale of the down-and-out scholar who pocketed his pride and made house-to-house calls in search of work. He knocked at the farmhouse door of the meanest old lady in (name of local town). She not only set him to work, she followed him about all day to make sure he wasn't idle for a moment. When at last mealtime came round, she grudgingly presented him with a slice of bread and butter and a large plate, in the middle of which was a very, very small spot of honey. Undefeated, the scholar

looked up at her with polite interest and said, 'I see, madam, that you keep a bee.'

"That's the kind of thing I usually think of later and wish I'd said. A speech is too often the kind of thing you think of earlier and wish you hadn't said . . ."

MERGER OR TAKEOVER "Harmony needs two voices. There's always a common gain in what scientists call 'symbiosis', defined in my dictionary as a 'mutually beneficial partnership'. What plain folk call 'fair give-and-take on both sides'.

"A widower friend of mine was sixty-five this year. Jim's still a handsome fellow, grey-haired but fit, and never one to say much until he has something worth saying. Last week we were on the golf course when, after a silent hour or so of concentrated play, he said, 'By the way, I'm getting married again.' When he told me his fiancée's name I was a bit shocked. I said, 'But, Jim, she's only twenty-four and you're sixty-five.' He didn't answer. I said, 'I must be honest with you, old friend. I don't believe in these May-December marriages.' He still didn't answer. I said, 'After all, December is going to find in May all the sweet glory and freshness of springtime. But, Jim, what is May going to find in December?' And Jim said, 'Christmas.'

"To partners forming an alliance in trust and joint purpose, I can add little to that as a wish. Have a merry Christmas and a happy New Era . . ."

DISPOSAL OF A LOSSMAKER "Sentimental attachment has a sadly limited life in the competitive world.

"Like the classic little story of the desperate wife who tells her priest she wants a divorce. The good clergyman says, 'Have you forgotten? When you married this man it was for life.' She says, 'I know, I know—but for the past eight years he hasn't shown any.'

"Slimmer and fitter, we carry the signs of vitality and the prospect of a lively future . . ."

PERSEVERANCE UNDER ATTACK "A determination to stand fast in hostile circumstances is a quality that may at first be condemned as stubborn but which must, when steadily and good-naturedly maintained, eventually win respect.

"They still tell the story in the southern West Virginia valleys about a local blue-blood's first bid to become a state senator. Some of the diehard miners at the rally thought him too intellectual and too aristocratic. 'Vote for you?' jeered one red-faced pitworker. 'Why, I'd sooner vote for the Devil!' 'Fair enough!' called out the candidate, 'But in the event of your friend not running, may I have your support?'

"Never give up the ship, or, as someone else once put it, 'The opera's not over till the fat lady sings' . . ."

SOFT ANSWERS "Answering harsh criticism with instant protest may seem justified but it's often a knee-jerk reaction without regard to a desired result. Someone attacks you and your instinctive response may be angry, but will that bring you the conclusion you really want? Doesn't it pay to pause a moment to see if you can produce a more profitable response, a gentle answer that loses you nothing in terms of self-esteem?

"True story: The great photographer, Josef Karsh, was dining at Le Cirque in New York when Marlene Dietrich swept in. She had every eye upon her as she paused at Karsh's table, turned to him with disdain and proclaimed for all to hear, 'Those photos you've just taken of me are atrocious! Hideous! You used to be the best but now you're pathetic. I remember the first pictures you ever did of me, they were fantastically beautiful.' There was a stunned silence in the restaurant, during which everyone there heard Karsh say, 'Yes, they were beautiful pictures, my dear, but you must bear in mind that I was twenty years younger then.'

"Diplomacy need not be soft. And answering an insult with charm can produce a far more desirable effect . . ."

PARTNERSHIP "Sometimes one and one can add up to a lot more than two. Partners can inspire each other, even compete with each other, achieving far greater results as a team than either of them could do alone. But it's also important to understand the limitations of partnership.

"There's a vintage story the French tell up in Montreal. One partner says, 'Our new secretary is such a sexy woman, in fact she makes love better than my wife.' The next day his partner says,

'You're right, she's sexy—and, mon Dieu, does she know how to make love! But not better than your wife.'
"That's what I call putting the caring into sharing . . ."

COURTESY "There are many kinds of human behavior which, although not essential to survival, make living pleasurable. Good humor, good fellowship, sympathy, patience, diplomacy and, perhaps the one that is becoming the rarest of these, old-fashioned courtesy.

"Remember the man on the bus who stood up to give a woman his seat and she was so surprised she fainted. When she came round she said, 'Thank you' and he fainted.

"I'm grateful that courtesy's not in short supply here tonight . . ."

MAKING NEW FRIENDS "Friendship can be based on long acquaintance or it can be instantaneous, forming itself quite involuntarily.

"She was standing, waiting for a bus, in a very tight skirt. And she had to wait quite a long time because, well, you don't find many buses in tight skirts, do you? She knew that when the bus came along she'd have trouble climbing aboard in her very tight skirt. So she reached stealthily behind her and loosened the zipper. When the bus arrived, the man behind her in the line picked her up and put her on it. She said, 'How dare you do that!' And he said, 'Well, after you opened my fly, I thought we were friends.'

"From the warmth of your welcome, I think we are friends too . . ."

FITTING IN WITH A NEW CROWD "Some of us feel quite apprehensive about joining a new company and being accepted by new associates. It never turns out to be as difficult as we feared, except in the most abnormal circumstances.

"Picture if you will a small garrison of GIs in a distant desert outpost. A new Army chaplain arrives and goes at once to report to the CO. 'Good morning, Colonel, I'm the new chaplain.' The colonel says, 'Welcome to the regiment, you'll soon fit in, we have an excellent social life. Every Wednesday night all the boys get together in the mess, drink until they're sick as pigs and fall over,

you'll love Wednesday nights.' The chaplain says, 'Actually, colonel, I don't approve of drinking.' The CO says, 'No matter, forget Wednesdays, you'll love Thursdays. That's the night we run our poker school.' 'No, sir, I never gamble.' 'Never mind, you'll enjoy Fridays. Every Friday night a bunch of the local native girls come over, ravishing women, all night long.' 'No, sir! I don't do that sort of thing!' 'Good God, man, are you gay?' 'Certainly not!' 'Oh, then you won't enjoy Saturday nights either.'

"I did say abnormal circumstances. Ours are closer to normality . . ."

GETTING TO KNOW YOU "Now I never like to take a person at face value. Before I begin to deal with anybody new, I like to know something about their personal history, so that I'm not coping with an unknown quantity or quality.

"Although I once made the mistake of playing darts for money with a stranger who told me he was new to the dartboard. I explained the rules and he proceeded to beat me hollow. I said, 'I thought you told me you were new to darts?' He said, 'No, new to the dartboard. I was a prisoner-of-war for three years and all we had was a set of darts. So I used to practice by pinning flies to the wall.' I said, 'But surely their blood made a bit of a mess,' and he said, 'Not if you pin 'em by one leg.'

"On this occasion my spies have got me better prepared to meet you tonight . . ."

OVER-DEDICATION TO WORK "When people are described as workaholics the term is seldom used pejoratively. We see hard work as admirable and so it is, but it can be overdone.

"Sam, for example. Sam's a buyer, always on the road for a week at a time, buying, buying. In the course of his work he meets some attractive girls. One week his wife gets a telegram: 'DEAR SADIE, CAN'T COME HOME, I'M STILL BUYING, LOVE— SAM.' Five weeks in a row she gets that same telegram: 'DEAR SADIE, CAN'T COME HOME, I'M STILL BUYING, LOVE— SAM.' The sixth week she sends him a telegram: 'DEAR SAM, BETTER COME HOME BECAUSE I'M SELLING WHAT YOU'RE BUYING.'

"The rewards of hard work are many but overwork can turn them into penalties . . ."

SELF-DISCLOSURE "A speaker is always in danger of telling his audience more about himself than he means to. But isn't that true of all of us in our everyday encounters? Don't you find people reveal their true interests in what they say and how they say it without even realizing it?

"I was in a saloon in (name of local town) when a priest walked in and said, 'Can anyone direct me to St. Broderick's Church?' And the barmaid said, 'Your best way is to cross over by Tower Records, turn right at the Next shop, left at Dirty Den's Disco and you can't miss it.' The poor clergyman didn't know what she was talking about. Then the old souse next to me put down his seventh glass of beer and said, 'Listen, Rev, you want to go left out of here to the Red Lion Tavern, cross over to Duffy's, pass the liquor store and turn right at the Tommy's Bar and Grill.' Well, I just had to speak up. I said, 'Father, the best route to take is left at the Pink Pussycat Massage parlor, right at the Naked City Striperama, past the Adult Book Shop, take the alley by the X-Rated movie theater and it's opposite Fanlight Fannie's Singles Club.' And he said, 'Thank God you were here, my son, or I'd never have found it.'

"As you can tell, I'm not always on my guard about giving myself away—and on this occasion my defenses are down again . . ."

DISCOVERY "Some men get discovered, others just get found out.

"There's the classic case of the policeman on night duty in the dead of winter who left his beat to run back to his house, throw a pebble at his bedroom window until his wife looked out, and then call out, 'Sorry to wake you, love, but I left my heavy overcoat over the bedside chair. Throw it down to me, will you?' And she did and he put it on and felt much warmer. Then a bit later he stopped into the station for a cup of coffee and as he walked in, one of the men said, 'Hey George, how long have you been a Sergeant?'

"Generally, though, worthwhile discoveries are not things that just turn up, they have to be turned up . . ."

PERSONAL REASONS "Often when we suspect people of having ulterior motives, what they really have are simply good reasons we haven't thought of.

"*Last week I asked my teenage son if I could borrow his record-player for the evening. He said, 'Certainly, dad—do you want some rock and roll?' I said, 'No, some peace and quiet.'*

"I think I've an equally reasonable purpose for being here now . . ."

"*Like the 60-year-old lady who went to the doctor for some birth-control pills. He said, 'But why on earth do you think you need them?' She said, 'A pill a day gets rid of my headache.' He said, 'But that's impossible.' She said, 'Listen to me—I live with my grand-daughter, a stunningly beautiful 16-year-old girl. Every morning we have breakfast together and, when she's not looking, I take one pill and pop it in her tea. Believe me, it gets rid of my headache.'*

"Perhaps you'll allow me to share a headache cure with you . . ."

AWKWARD SITUATIONS "In your/my position, it's necessary to develop a skill at handling difficult relationships.

"*I recall a gorgeous stewardess who had two over-amorous men on the same flight to New York, both pestering her for a date, begging for her address, phone number, everything. One even went so far as to pull his New York apartment key out of his pocket, jot down his address and beg her to 'Please come and see me around nine tonight—I'll be all ready for you, baby. Candlelight and wine and my circular waterbed!' She gave him the sweetest smile. Then she made her way to the front of the plane where her other admirer was breathing heavily, slipped him the key and the address and murmured, 'Nine o'clock, don't be late!'"I bet that first fellow felt like a fool. I certainly did when I showed up at his apartment.*

"But it's the stewardess who is our shining example. How can we fail to admire the way she disengaged herself from that unwelcome situation without actually offending anyone . . ."

INTERNATIONAL COMPETITION "Are the British sufficiently competitive? Well, the famous British reserve, that self-effacing modesty, seems to evaporate very rapidly whenever anyone suggests that another nation can boast more beautiful women.

"*A subject once discussed by an Arab, and Englishman and a Swede. The Arab said, 'Arabian women are the most beautiful* in the world—the sensuous walk, the demure gaze over the yashmak—why, when I leave home every day I kiss each of my wives in turn. And when I return from my day's work, only one of them is in bed waiting for me. I tell you this to show how beautifully they agree between themselves who shall enjoy my attentions.' The Englishman said, 'So sorry to disagree, but English women are definitely the most beautiful—the complexion of a rose, the grace, poise and style—why, when I leave home every day I give my wife a peck on the cheek. And when I return from my day's work, the house is spotless, the children are bathed and my supper is on the table. I tell you this to show you how beautifully she accomplishes her wifely duties.' The Swede said, 'You pardon me, but Swedish women are the most beautiful—plump, rosy-cheeked, blonde—why, when I am leaving my home every day, I am giving my wife a slap on the bottom. And when I return, the bottom, it is still trembling. And I tell you this not to give you the idea that Swedish women have fat bums, but to show you what a short working day we have in Sweden.'

"Patriotism takes pride in very different national assets. And companies too vary in their reasons for feeling proud . . ."

Note: This is a carefully phrased and detailed story. If you decide to use it, it's necessary to study its repetitions and variations and memorize them thoroughly. With the right audience, it's a big, long laugh, the kind I put next to closing.

POSSESSIONS "It's been said that the man who has everything is probably not married to the woman who wants everything. Such a man is widely envied today. More and more it seems that material gain is placed before spiritual. The philosophy of the Yuppie could be expressed as 'I own, therefore I am.'

"I heard of one young, upwardly mobile executive in San Francisco who was speeding in his treasured Porsche when he crashed. A traffic cop pulled him from the blazing wreck and said, 'Keep still, I'll get an ambulance.' But all the Yuppie could say was, 'My Porsche, my Porsche, my Porsche . . . !' The policeman said, 'That's the least of your worries, you've lost your left arm.' And the Yuppie said, 'My Rolex, my Rolex, my Rolex . . . !'

"Worldly goods are all very well but this room is filled with an intangible though far greater wealth—good fellowship . . ."

126

THE LEGAL MIND "What's that cynical old definition of a lawyer? He's a man who gets two people to strip for a fight and then runs off with their clothes. How unkind—yet it rings a bell for each of us. The legal profession could do with an improved image.

"*I'm rather fond of the classic story about the dying millionaire who called three men to his death-bed: his clergyman, his doctor and his lawyer. The old man said, 'They say you can't take it with you but I'm going to try. Here are three fireproof envelopes, each of them containing $50,000, one apiece. Take them and keep them until the day of my funeral—and just before they lower my coffin, throw them in with me.' And so it was done on the funeral day, but on the road back in the black limousine, the clergyman made a confession. He said, 'I took $10,000 for the Church Restoration Fund and only threw in $40,000.' The doctor said, 'To be frank, I took $20,000 for new hospital equipment and only threw in $30,000.' And the lawyer said, 'I'm ashamed of you, gentlemen. I threw in a check for the full amount.'*"

SELLING TOO HARD "We have to guard against stretching the truth too far—it may snap back.

"*As in the old classic about the matchmaker who takes a young suitor to meet a prospective bride and her family. As they're leaving, the matchmaker says, 'Aren't they wonderful? What an honor to become part of such a family! Cultured people, dignified, educated, full of honor and integrity—and did you see their silverware? Pure sterling!' The young man says, 'Ah, but perhaps they only borrowed it to make a good impression.' And the matchmaker says, 'Are you crazy? Who would lend anything to those thieves?'*

"A good product doesn't sell itself, it just deserves an equally good salesman . . ."

RELAXATION "Stress is not only a personal enemy, it's an enemy to good business too. A decision taken under pressure can go wrong. Let me tell you what my doctor says—it's pretty good advice when you think about it. He says the best time to relax is when you haven't got time to relax.

"*I heard of a Rhode Island doctor who told an overworked priest, 'Go to Miami, put away your Roman collar, forget the church for two months and have some really relaxing fun.' A week later the priest is wearing a Gautier suit, sipping a dry Martini in the hottest club on the beach when a cute little topless waitress says, 'Hi there, Father O'Malley!' He says, 'How do you know me?' She says, 'I'm Sister Theresa, we go to the same doctor.'*

"If the job gets one hundred per cent and there's nothing good left for you, pretty soon there's nothing good left for the job . . ."

COINCIDENCE "It's only in fiction that coincidences seem unnatural. When they occur in life, we're hardly surprised.

"Only last week two friends of mine were walking down the street when one said, 'There's my wife and my girlfriend talking to each other!' And the other one said, 'Small world, isn't it?'

"I think it's a lucky coincidence that you and I are here at the same time . . ."

CURIOSITY "In the words of Ralph Waldo Emerson, 'Curiosity is lying in wait for every secret.' Some mysteries are irresistible.

"As in the classic about the honeymoon couple who bought a talking parrot in a bazaar. The damn thing kept up a running commentary on everything they were doing in bed. Finally the groom threw a bath towel over its cage and said, 'Shut up or we'll sell you to a zoo!' Next morning they were packing and couldn't get the big suitcase shut. He said, 'Darling, you get on top and I'll try. No, that's not working—let me get on top and you try.' She said, 'That's not working either, dearest. Why don't we both get on top?' And the parrot yanked off the towel and said, 'Zoo or no zoo, this I've got to see!'

"I feel just as curious as that parrot and just as determined to know the answers that await us . . ."

ANTICIPATING NEEDS "What you need today may not be what you will need tomorrow. It's a good idea to reconsider your priorities regularly.

"Remember the drunk weeping to his friend, 'I did a terrible thing. I sold my wife to a guy for a bottle of Scotch.' His friend said, 'That is terrible. And now that she's gone you wish you had her back.' And the drunk said, 'Damn right, I'm thirsty again.'

"He didn't anticipate requirements. I just hope that I've anticipated yours . . ."

SPECIALIZATION "We should all stick to what we do best, but if what we do isn't the best, it's better not to claim credit for it.

"There's a classic tale about three specialists—a doctor, a civil engineer and a politician—all discussing the beginning of Creation. The doctor says, 'It was obviously a surgical job. The Bible says Eve was made by removing a rib from Adam.' The engineer says, 'That came later, before that it was an engineering job. For in six days the earth was created out of chaos.' 'Aha!' says the politician. 'But who created the chaos?'

"So what can we claim to have created here? . . ."

ADVICE "The best time to give advice to your children is while they're still young enough to believe you know what you're talking about. By the time they're twenty, they think you're a fool. By the time they're forty, they're surprised how much you've learned in the meantime.

"An old story but still a great one by the French film-maker Jean Renoir tells of the Sorbonne graduate getting some astute business advice from his old man: 'My boy, guard well the fingers of your right hand.' 'Why, mon pere?' 'It's like this—the little finger extends when you drink tea—this shows class. The third finger is for the wedding ring. The middle finger is for pleasure, the index finger is for turning the pages of our financial ledgers, and the thumb is for passing judgment, up or down.' The young man thought for a moment and then said, 'Papa, I understand all that except the part about the middle finger being for pleasure.' And the old man answered, 'Think, my boy, think! How else would you punch the cash register?'

"There are few points we can count off on *our* fingers . . ."

REVENGE "A gambling expert tells me that the longest odds in the world are those against getting even. But it's still tempting.

"Which recalls the classic instance of the two schoolboys who were always feuding and grew up to be bitter enemies. One entered the Navy and became an Admiral. The other entered the Church and in due time became a Bishop. Years later they met again on

*a Long Island railway platform. The Bishop, who had grown enor-
mously fat, walked up to the Admiral who was decked out in his
full official regalia, a uniform resplendent with decorations. He
said, 'Stationmaster, what time does the train leave for
Manhasset?' And the Admiral bowed and said, 'Any minute now,
madam, but in your condition you really shouldn't be travelling.'*

"The truth is that time spent in getting even is far better
used in getting ahead . . ."

FAITH "Peter De Vries once said, 'It takes a lot more faith to live
this life without faith than with it.' And faith, once accepted into
the heart, carries the mind with it.

*"Like Mrs. Murphy who said to her parish priest, 'I hear you're
away to Rome, Father. Would you say a prayer for me that I'll get
pregnant at last and raise a family?' The clergyman said, 'I'll do
more than that, Mrs. Murphy. I'll light a candle in St. Peter's
Basilica.' Eight years later he returned to (name of local town) and
the first he saw was Mrs. Murphy. She kissed his hand and said,
'You're a living saint, Father. The three boys are at school, the twins
are in the stroller, and the two girls are playing in the yard.' He
said, 'Glory be to God! And where's your husband?' She said, 'He's
gone off to Rome to blow out the candle.'*

"Good luck and faith may sometimes be confused but we do
best when we are blessed with both . . ."

CIRCUMSTANCES "It's been said that whether circumstances
make one bitter or better depends entirely on the letter 'I'.

*"The great humorist Will Rogers took the better view. He was
delivering one of his famous topical monologues in the great
Ziegfeld Follies on an evening during World War I when a grim-
looking female in the balcony screamed, 'Why aren't you in the
armed forces?' Rogers gazed upwards at his heckler until everyone
had turned to look at her, then he drawled, 'Ma'am, it's for the
same reason you ain't in the Ziegfeld Follies—physical
disabilities.'*

"As for all of us, in sporting terms, it's 'horses for courses' . . ."

HYPOCRISY "A hypocrite is someone who slaps you on the back
in front of your face, and slaps you in the face behind your back.

130

"Like the hypocritical wheeler-dealer who once told Mark Twain, 'Before I kick the bucket I intend to make a pilgrimage to the Holy Land, climb to the very top of Mount Sinai and read the Ten Commandments out loud.' Twain said, 'I've got a better idea. Why don't you stay right here where you are and keep them?'

"Honesty is still the best policy. Of course, there are fewer policy holders than there used to be. . . ."

CONCEIT "A vain man thinks he's flattering his wife when he congratulates her on her choice of husband. Thank goodness there's always a pin for such a balloon.

"A notoriously self-centered comedian was due to be the Guest of Honor at yet another show business dinner for one of the many charities he supports. He stood in front of the mirror in the men's room, adjusting his black bow tie, pinching his cheeks to heighten the color and generally checking out his appearance. Then he said to the attendant, 'How many really important men do you think there are in the banquet hall tonight?' And the attendant said, 'One less than you think.'

"Looking around me, I have exactly the same feeling . . ."

INTERPRETATIONS "Whatever action we take we should always bear in mind its possible ambiguities. Can it be misunderstood? And could that misunderstanding arise from our previous behavior?

"About a year ago I had to complain angrily to the manager of our local dry cleaners. I can't have left her with a very favorable impression of me. Then last week I put a red ballpoint pen in the breast pocket of my white shirt and forgot to put the cap on it. It made a ghastly scarlet stain with a dark center all over the pocket and my wife said, 'It won't wash out, I'll try the cleaners.' The manager took a long, slow look at the shirt and then looked sideways at my wife with a furtive grin and murmured, 'Good shot.'

"At least let's make it clear that our aims are not criminal . . ."

POSITIVE THINKING "I've heard it said that positive something is better than negative nothing. I'm all for the power of positive thinking, but some of its optimistic language, though it trips off the tongue, can also trip you up.

"I took a computer course recently in distinguished company. Along with several leading businessmen of my age, I sat like a new boy in school and grappled with the jargon familiar to all end-users but like Martian to me. Our instructor fairly radiated positive thinking. He thought and spoke only in terms of the impossibility of failure and the certainty of success. We were given a test in data processing to complete and, as we did so, one or two of us began to discuss the problems we'd encountered. The instructor wasn't having that. He said, 'Let me make one thing perfectly clear, gentlemen! In the world of computer programming there are no such things as problems—only opportunities!' There was a pause, and then a very eminent executive in the far corner said very gently, 'In that case, I wonder if you'd give me some help with an insurmountable opportunity?'

"It's fine to have one eye on the objective providing you keep an objective view . . ."

LATERAL THINKING "The ability either to see a gap in the market, or to spot a dormant public demand that needs awakening, or visualize the application of a familiar tool to a new and unfamiliar task—this is the kind of thinking which breaks out of the habitual and into the unconventional. Why is it so rare? Most of us use this trick of informal figuring when we're at play—doing crosswords, playing cards, even cracking jokes. We use it whenever we solve a logical puzzle, like G-H-O-T-I spells 'fish'. If you don't know why G-H-O-T-I spells 'fish', I'll explain in just a moment.

"This capacity for identifying unusual connections was the very test used on the final applicants for the job as head chef at the Ritz Hotel. The general manager had reduced his list to three, an Englishman, a Scotsman and an Irishman. (When this joke happened the Welshman was on holiday.) He said, 'Look, gentlemen, your qualifications are identical and I can't separate you, so we must use a tie-breaker. I've put three objects on this table. I want each of you to pick the odd one out and give me your reasons.' And on the table were a cabbage, a potato and a knife. The English contender said, 'The odd one out is the knife because the other two are

edible.' The Scotsman said, 'Aye, it's the knife all right but not for that reason. It's because the cabbage and the potato are vegetable and the knife is mineral.' Murphy took a look and said, 'It's the cabbage.' 'The cabbage? Why the cabbage?' 'You can make chips with the other two.'

"As to why G-H-O-T-I spells 'fish', it's just another example of spotting the connection, this time between English spelling and pronunciation. In the word 'cough' the G-H are pronounced F, 'cough'. In the word 'women', the O is pronounced as I, 'women'. In the word 'motion', the T-I are pronounced SH, 'motion'. That's an F, an I and a SH and that spells 'fish'. Which sends my mind leaping sideways to this thought . . ."

SELFISHNESS "The humorist Roger Price wrote a book called *Me First*. In it he coined one of my favorite ambiguities: 'When it comes to giving to others, I stop at nothing.' Of course, there are certain circumstances in which total self-absorption is understandable.

"Consider a fellow called Henry whose doctor tells him he has only eight hours to live. Henry goes home in a state of shock and tells his wife, 'I've only got seven hours to live.' (It's taken him an hour to get home.) For the next sixty minutes they're weeping, lamenting, then he says, 'Wait a minute! I've only got six hours left—let's do something worthwhile with my last six hours.' She says, 'What?' He says, 'Let's make love.' So they go upstairs and enjoy an hour of passion. Harry's exhausted, he sleeps for an hour. Then he wakes up, it's 10 PM, he says, 'I've got four hours left—let's make love again!' Once more sixty minutes of passion go by and once more he crashes out, shattered. He sleeps for an hour, wakes up at midnight, shakes his wife's arm and says, 'I've still got a couple of hours of life left—let's make love again.' And she says, 'Oh, come on, have some consideration! I've got to get up in the morning, you don't.'

"In most cases, however, we best serve ourselves by putting others first, be it the family, the company or the customer . . ."

ADVANCING THE CUSTOMERS' NEEDS "In politics, the public is divided into friends and enemies. In business, they're all customers. And what a customer thinks he needs is often less than we can sell him. It's just a matter of being alert to opportunity.

"Like the tattooist when a pretty punk rocker walked into his parlor said, 'Can you tattoo a wildcat on my knee?' And he said, 'We're having a sale on giraffes this week.'

"We too should aim as high as we possibly can . . ."

SPORTS CLASSICS

Every kind of sport has its comic legends and here are some stories that have proved their worth. It seems that golf attracts the greatest number of funny lines and anecdotes so "Golfing Gags" occupies the most space. But let's kick off with:

Football Stories

"I was telling my son that there's nothing certain in life. Then Harvard lost another game. (Use the name of any well-known losing football team.) I spend a lot of my time watching that team. My doctor told me to avoid excitement. They just spent ¢30,000 on ground improvements—turned the seats around to face the home team's goalposts.

"We got beaten by (Yale) last Saturday. One of our players went up to the referee and said, 'Can we have a new ball?' 'What's wrong with the one you've got?' 'Yale's playing with it.'

"But we've got a winning team here today . . ."

FOLLOWING A BIG GAME "It was sold out, of course, with the usual ticket scalpers trying to make a killing. I heard one guy saying, 'Fifty bucks for a football game? I could get a woman for that.' And the scalper said, 'Yes, but you won't get four quarters and a brass marching band at halftime.'

"Denver was playing Boston and the referee came from Florida. He called the two captains together before the game and said, 'Look, men, before the afternoon's over I think it's going to snow, so what do you say we play the overtime first?'

"Taking a tip from that, I'll use my overtime right now . . ."

134

"I play for our local team in (name of home town). Best result so far was losing to the senior citizens by thirteen points. They beat us 12—zero.

"One of our supporters is a dairy farmer who always brings along his very plain unmarried sister. I've noticed how he always likes to stand near the 50-yard line while she takes up her position directly behind our goal posts. Last week I asked him why his sister prefers to stand there and he said, 'She ain't no beauty, and this is the only time she ever sees men running right at her.'

"Like so many things, it all depends on the point of view . . ."

"Then there's the coach who says the team's taking art lessons so they can draw bigger crowds.

"And they are trying to boost attendance. Before each home game they have two hundred policemen outside the ground throwing rowdies in. But I make donations to the club each season. I put one dollar in an envelope and sent it off last year. I got a very nice letter back from the Coach saying, 'Thank you for the dollar you sent. Which two players do you want?'

"Why, it took nearly twice that much to lure me here tonight . . ."

"My old football injury is acting up again. It happened a few years ago. I was watching *the Superbowl* and I accidentally cut my thumb on a can of Budweiser. Of course, some supporters are even more dedicated than I am.

"One loyal (name of team) supporter went to the coach and said, 'I've spent my entire life devoted to the team and I've not long to go. When that Great Referee in the Sky blows the final whistle for me, I want to be cremated. And I want my ashes scattered over the stadium ground.' The coach said, 'Come on man, you know very well that we don't allow spectators on the field at kickoff. Have you thought about being mummified?' The old chap said, 'What a grand idea! I'll have myself preserved and you can put me in my old seat on the fifty-yard line every Saturday!' And, believe it or not, that's just what happened. He died, the taxidermist did his stuff, and there he was the following Saturday afternoon, stuffed and mummified, looking better than usual, sitting in his usual

JUST SAY A FEW WORDS

seat at *(club) Stadium, as usual. And the team played up to their
normal standard, as usual. And he left at half-time, as usual.*
  "And it's time the speaker offered his thanks, as usual . . ."

*KEEPING YOUR EYE ON THE BALL (AFTER A LEG-
PULLING INTRODUCTION)* "I don't know. Having you warm up
an audience is a little like having Yasser Arafat warm up a bagel.
But in football, you learn to take a few kicks, fouls and penalties.
Most importantly, as in life, you learn not to take your eye off the
ball. When its direction changes, you change with it. Every good
businessman knows if you're not flexible to market forces, you lose
profits. As in football, to win you must adapt to every changing
situation.

Golfing Gags

"Someone defined a golf ball as a sphere made of rubber bands
wound up about as tensely as the man trying to hit it. Of course,
that was before they found new ways to make them. I've bought
some of these "longer distance balls". You can't believe how much
further out of bounds they'll go. To give you some idea of how
they've improved my game, I've got the only caddy on the course
in a snorkel and flippers.
  *"I'm not as bad as (name) though. He drove four successive
balls into the water and then blew his top. He snatched his bag
from the caddie and threw the whole lot into the pond—bag,
clubs, balls and all. Then he said, 'Now I'm going to jump in there
and drown myself.' The caddie said, 'I doubt it.' 'What do you
mean, you doubt it?' The caddy said, 'You never have learned to
keep your head down.'*
  "Well, I think I can be more tactful than that . . ."

"Every golfer has his excuses for playing badly, even Bob Hope,
who blamed his disappointing stroke play in his last charity classic on a man holding the cue cards in the wrong order.
  *"Hope tells the story that his doctor told him he was over-
worked for a man in his eighties and needed a complete rest— and
that included giving up golf. Hope decided to give up his doctor
instead. He tried a second opinion and a third, and on the fourth*

136

try he found a doctor who told him he could play eighteen holes whenever he felt like it. Hope says he actually hugged the man and said, 'Thanks, doc, just for that I'll remember you in my will.' And the doctor said, 'In that case, play thirty-six.'

"Personally I think there's only one psychologically right time to give up golf. It's when your putt goes further than your drive. And this may be the psychologically right time to say this . . ."

"Every golf ball has 332 dimples. Easy for me to remember—the way I'm playing lately that's one dimple per stroke. And when you're off your game, the least thing can distract you.

"The last game I played with (name) was a bit temperamental. And as if things weren't tense enough, the caddie developed a deafening case of hiccups. On the sixteenth, (name) sliced his drive way out of bounds, turned to the caddie and said, 'That's thanks to you and your damned hiccups!' The caddie said, 'But I didn't hiccup then, sir.' (name) said, 'That's just the point— I had allowed for it!'

"And now I must ask you to make allowances for me . . ."

"I'm, not saying (name) is a bad golfer, but he's stood in more sand than Lawrence of Arabia. When he lowers his head, he's not just putting—he's praying.

"Rather like the tale about the priest and the rabbi playing at (name of local course). The priest made a small silent prayer before each putt and he was sinking them from every corner of the green. The rabbi was rattled. Half in jest he said, 'If you taught me that little prayer of yours, do you think my putts would start dropping too?' The priest said, 'Frankly, no.' 'Why not?' 'Because you're a lousy putter.'

"However, if you have prayers, prepare to say them now . . ."

"I like to watch golfers on the links and try to figure out their relationships.

"For instance, you can always spot an employee who's playing with his boss. The employee is the player who gets a hole-in-one and says, 'Oops!'

"The secret of good golf is threefold: hit the ball hard, straight, and not too often. That's fine until you find yourself playing a hole that refuses to let you do either the second or the third.

"*A veteran golfer I knew at (name of local club) was constantly defeated by the 13th hole. That hole always got the better of him, always made him finish up one or two strokes over par. He told his wife, 'When I die, I want to get my own back on that 13th hole if it kills me! Promise me you'll have my ashes scattered all over that damned 13th hole.' And sure enough, when he died, after the funeral, his wife solemnly scattered his ashes all over the fairway—and the wind blew them out of bounds.*"

"Sometimes you can't win—but you've got to try . . ."

"I've heard that Pebble Beach is one of the toughest around and I can't disagree. I mean, how often have you seen a sandtrap with headstones? Consequently, it attracts quite a lot of visitors who fancy a challenge.

"*One out-of-town visitor finished his game and he's standing in the showers, musing on his handicap, when he hears a group of lady members outside the shower, laughing. I wish they were here tonight. Anyway, he realizes that they're all getting undressed and that he's in the ladies' shower. So he covers his head with a towel, rushes out past the three women and makes his escape. The first woman said, 'Who was that? It wasn't my husband.' The second woman said, 'No, you're right, it wasn't. And it wasn't my husband either.' And the third woman said, 'He isn't even a member of the club.'*

"It's not only a nice story, it's a relief that religion doesn't come into it. I've got a friend who says nine holes are enough for him—he usually plays four and falls down five. But that's what every game is all about—the challenge . . ."

"*My friend's caddy got on his nerves one afternoon. He said to the man, 'Are you anxious to get home or what? Every time I hit the ball, you look at your watch.' The caddy said, 'It's not a watch, it's a compass.'*

"I get my warning signs when you look at your watches . . ."

"Jack Lemmon was in a talkative mood during a match with a tight-lipped Sean Connery. The more Jack chattered, the quieter Sean became. Just as Sean was driving off from the 5th, Jack launched into another topic and the ball fell short into a bunker. 'Tough,' said Jack, 'but there's an even worse trap than that on this course.' Sean said, 'I know—why don't you shut it?'

"Sean likes the tale of Jesus and Moses coming to earth incognito to play a game at Turnberry. They're on the wrong side of the pond on a short hole and Jesus says to his caddy, 'Give me a seven-iron.' Moses says, 'Why not? Jack Nicklaus did it.' He gives it an Almighty swing, if you'll excuse the expression, and SPLOSH! The ball's in the water. He says, 'Moses, do me a favor and fetch my ball.' So Moses parts the waters and brings back the ball. Again Jesus lines up a shot with the seven-iron, again Moses says, 'You'll never clear that pond with a seven- iron,' and again Jesus says, 'Why not? Jack Nicklaus did it.' He swings again and SPLOSH! Ball's back in the water. 'Moses, fetch the ball again, please.' Moses says, 'No, it's your ball, you get it.' So Jesus walks out onto the water. One of the caddies says, 'I don't believe this game. Who does he think he is—Jesus Christ?' And Moses says, 'No, Jack Nicklaus.'

"Some golfers have the perfect cure for a stiff neck: rub it with alcohol—from the inside.

"On a bitterly cold day last November four of our oldest members went out into the winds, determined not to give up their twice-weekly foursome. Off they roared from the 1st tee, repeating their pet insults, making crazy bets, stopping after each four strokes to pass round the hip flasks. By the 18th green the four of them were so sozzled their knees were bending both ways. Besides which, they were all even. The entire match depended on whether or not one of the oldest of these four alcoholic grandads could sink a fifteen-foot putt uphill. He balanced himself very gingerly and prepared to make the putt, at which point a big red fox with a bushy tail flew from behind a clump of gorse, dashed between the old fellow's legs with an earsplitting howl, leaped off into the rough and vanished. Without batting an eyelid, the old boy calmly putted his ball into the cup. The other three couldn't get over it. They congratulated him all the way back to the locker room. They said, 'You're a marvel. Imagine sinking a difficult putt like that

even though a damn great fox ran between your legs.' And the old fellow focussed his eyes and said, 'Hell, you don't mean that was a real fox?'

"Tonight, nothing's going to put me off my stroke either . . ."

"Another golfer said he once played eighteen holes at Palm Springs with the legendary Arnold Palmer. As the round ended he asked anxiously, 'What do you think of my game?' Palmer said, 'Not bad but I still prefer golf.'

"My friend Bob's favorite tale was of when he took his wife out for the first time. He told her to tee off and she said, 'I can't—those men in front are looking at me.' So Bob yelled, 'Hey, fellers! Don't look!' One of the players looked at his friend and said, 'What did he say?' His friend said, 'He said, "Don't look"' and the other guy said, 'Why? What are they going to do?'"

"I once asked a great golfer friend, 'What was your lowest score?' He said, 'Fifty-four.' 'And your highest?' He said, 'Two hundred and ninety-eight.' I said, 'What happened?' He said, 'I used a ball.' I said, 'What's the longest ball you ever hit?' He said, 'Three thousand miles. It went through the window of a plane.' Despite his magical skills, he confessed that he'd never attained the golfer's Holy Grail—the hole-in-one.

"Like that appalling golfer who swore, 'I'd give anything for it'—and there on his shoulder appeared a tiny Devil who said, 'If I grant you a hole-in-one, will you agree to give up ten years of your sex life?' This terrible golfer said, 'Anything! It's my life's ambition.' And with that he drove off down the fairway, his ball hit a rock, bounced off a tree, and rolled into the cup. 'Let me do it again!' he yelled and the Devil said, 'It'll cost you ten more years of your sex life!' 'It's a deal!'—and he holed another in one at the second— and another at the third—a world record! And the Devil met him behind the clubhouse and said, 'You've lost thirty years of sex, my friend, I hope it was worth it. Now for the details—what's your name?' And the golfer said, 'Father O'Malley.'

"I'd love to sink a ball in one but I wouldn't sacrifice this evening for it . . ."

"I wasn't playing at my best the other day and the caddy I had was worse than useless. I said, 'You must be the worst caddy in the world.' And he said, 'No, that would be too much of a coincidence.' What do you tip a man like that?

"As I was leaving I said to the pro, 'That caddy is a cocky swine. You were watching my game—what do you think I should give him?' He said, 'Your clubs.'

"(Name) never cheats. He just makes his nines upside down. You might say he plays by numbers—he sets to, yells 'Fore!', takes six and puts down five. I think fiddling his score has become too much of a habit. Last week he got a hole-in-one and put down a zero.

"And he'll make any excuse for playing off-form. I took him out to a new country club for a game the other week. I teed off, then he took a wild swing at his ball and missed by a mile. He tried again and again and each time he missed it. I was embarrassed, he wasn't. He turned to me and said, 'It's a good thing I discovered this early in the game. This course is at least two inches lower than the one I usually play on.'

"I have a similar problem—the IQ in this room is higher than I'm used to . . ."

"I never really mean to cheat at golf. It's just that I play for my health and a low score makes me feel better. But just now and then comes that incredible stroke of luck that makes all the suffering worthwhile.

"It would have been a real triumph except that I was playing with (name). I stepped up to the tee, drove off and got a hole-in-one. Then he stepped up the tee and said, 'Okay, now I'll take my practice swing and then we'll start the game.'

"Okay, that was my practice joke, now let's start the speech . . ."

"There are two things I like to leave behind me when I walk onto the golf course—business worries and sarcasm.

"I had an office problem on my mind last Saturday and it was ruining my form. I said to my partner, 'Sorry, I'm not playing my

usual game.' He said, 'Ah, that accounts for it—what game do you usually play?'"

"They're saying golf is so popular it's replaced sex. Of course, it's the fellers who are over sixty who are saying it. But that's one of its joys—you can take it up at any time of life.

"I know a workaholic, efficiency-mad businessman in (name of local town) who finally had to retire and it's driving him crazy. It's driving his wife crazy too, so to get him out of the house, she buys him a beautiful set of clubs and a membership at the local club. He presents himself to the resident pro and says, 'Look, this game is a total mystery to me. What do I have to do?' The pro says, 'See that flag down there on the green? You hit the ball towards that flag.' The man picks out a club at random, swipes at the ball and by some miracle of chance it goes straight down the middle and rolls across the green till it stops two inches from the hole. The pro can't believe his eyes. The man says, 'What next?' The pro gulps and says, 'You're supposed to hit the ball into the cup.' And the businessman says, 'Now he tells me!'"

"Well, I think we're unexpectedly lucky too . . ."

"Mad about golf? If they were going to hang him, he'd ask the executioner to let him fake a couple of practice swings.

"Once in California I played with the most fanatical golfer I've ever met. We were just teeing off on the 15th where the green lies next to the main road. He was in the middle of his backswing when a row of funeral cars came past. He stopped, took off his cap, held it over his heart and bowed his head. I was impressed. I said, 'You're a man who shows real respect for the deceased.' He said, 'It's only fair. She was a good wife to me for 37 years.'"

"That's one kind of dedication. I'd like to make another . . ."

"In school we have the rule of three, in courtship the rule of two, in marriage the rule of one . . . and in golf, quite a number of unwritten rules. But everyone plays by them.

"I was in the locker room at (local) Golf Club when the old attendant there answered the phone. He heard a female voice say, 'Is my husband there?' He said, 'No, lady, he's not here.' She yelled, 'How can you say he's not there when I haven't even told you my

name?' And he said, 'Don't make no difference, lady. There ain't never nobody's husband here!'"

"It's a poor rule that won't work both ways. And an even poorer one that won't work our way. . . ."

Horse Racing

"In horse racing there's nothing as uncertain as a sure thing. And if you think there is, chances are you'll wind up getting nothing for something. Funny thing is though, every horse trainer and every bookie has a story about racing coincidences.

"*I was at the Kentucky Derby, having a quiet beer in the local pub, when I noticed three racehorses sitting in a corner of the bar, drinking Irish Coffee and reminiscing. The first one said, 'I was in the 5.15 at Upson Downs last month, lying fifth and not bothered, when a dog barked somewhere and startled me so much I put on a spurt and won by a length.' The second horse said, 'What a coincidence! I was taking it easy in the 2 o'clock at Belmont Park when the same thing happened. A dog barked, gave me a start and I shot ahead to win by a head.' The third horse said, 'I can't get over this! Didn't exactly the same thing happen to me in the 4.30 at Monmouth? I was noodling along in the rear—woof woof! I jumped so much I led the field and came in at eight to one.' Listening to all this was a greyhound, sipping a port and lemon. It sauntered over to the three horses and said, 'You're not going to believe this, but only last night I was running at Miami, the back marker, when suddenly I heard a horse whinny! It gave me such a shock I leapt into the lead!' And the first racehorse turned to the others and said, 'Isn't that incredible? A talking dog!'*

"I'm sorry, I'm afraid I've been lying to you. This actually happened at Yonkers Raceway in the clubhouse. . . ."

Boxing

"The chains of habit are too weak to be felt until they become too strong to be broken.

"*Like the old insomniac boxer who was allergic to sleeping pills. The doctor said, 'The old remedies are best. Just relax and start counting to a thousand.' The old boxer was back a week later. He said, 'It's no use, doctor. I keep jumping up at the count of nine.'*

"First we make our habits—and then our habits make us . . ."

Short Thoughts

If brevity is the soul of wit, these lines should provide every speaker with soul-food. None of them is offered as a knee-slapping bellylaugh. Their merit lies in their encapsulation of a truth, a smart observation or a humorous example and they are intended to promote smiles and nods rather than helpless mirth. Mind you, the occasional jokey joke sneaks in. I've used them to open a subject or wrap one up, and you'll find other applications, I'm sure. A Sales Director told me, "I need short and intelligent lines to sprinkle over my speech like sultanas in a cake." If you're reading this, my friend—happy sprinkling!

Advertising

Some of it doesn't make sense, like a falsie manufacturer advertising "Beware of Imitations".

I keep seeing ads for mouthwashes that guarantee to kill all germs. Who wants a mouthful of dead germs?

I have a friend in Public Relations whose honeymoon was a disaster. He just sat on the edge of the bed and told her how wonderful it was going to be.

Advice

I can offer lots of advice, good advice. Advice that's been passed down from generation to generation and never been used.

Don't try to keep up with the Joneses. Drag them down to your level, it's cheaper.

If you have a jar with a lid that's stuck, do you know the easiest way to get it open? Put it on the table and tell the kids to leave it alone.

If you can't give up sex, get married and taper off.

Age

It's so unfair. You no sooner get used to being middle-aged and you're old.

You know you're getting older when you decide to procrastinate but never seem to get around to it.

I tried life in the fast lane recently. Got a summons for obstructing traffic.

You know you're getting older when a four-letter word for something pleasurable two people can do in bed is R-E-A-D.

Argument

There's one sure way to stop a red-hot argument. Drop one cold fact on it.

My wife and I have resolved not to go to bed angry. As of now we've been awake three weeks.

Some say avoid arguments if possible. I say avoid them if impossible.

There are two sides to every argument until you take one.

Art

I told (name) I didn't understand modern art and he said it's easy.
If it hangs on a wall, it's a painting and if you can walk round
it, it's a sculpture.
I heard one woman in the gallery say, "That's a beautiful painting,"
and the woman next to her turned and said, "Oh, are you a rela-
tive too?"
An artist is known by the critics he praises.
Our local bar's full of artists but none of them can paint.

Average

I'd consider myself an average man if it weren't for the fact that
I consider myself an average man.
On average at age eighty-five there are sixty per cent more
women than men. But at that age, who cares?

Babies

A baby's like a new car. It has two-lung power, free squealing,
screamlined body, changeable seat covers and an easily flooded
carburetor.
She's not a great thinker. She keeps having a baby every year
because she doesn't want the youngest one to get spoiled.
Training babies is mostly a matter of pot luck.

Bachelors

I said, "Dad, should I marry a girl who can take a joke?" He said,
"Son, that's the only kind you'll get."
He's been single for years. Can't find someone who loves him as
much as he does.
He's a very lonely bachelor. Goes to women's prisons and volun-
teers for conjugal visits.
She reckons no man is good enough for her. She may be right. And
she may be left.

Beds

Nothing makes a lumpy mattress more comfortable than the ringing of an alarm clock.
Politics doesn't make strange bedfellows, marriage does.
The best time to put your children to bed is when you can.
My wife used to walk in her sleep, then we got a waterbed. Now she swims in her sleep.

Books

I know a publisher who begged (name of Hollywood beauty) to write her memoirs. She said, "Submit an outline and a couple of chapters and I'll think about it."
Never judge a book by its movie.
He said, "This encyclopedia will do half your work for you." I said, "Wonderful, I'll take two."
I was swindled last week—I bought a book called *How To Make It Big*. It was all about money.

Budget

These days the government spends as much accidentally as it did on purpose 30 years ago.
The good news is that the Budget is doing a lot for small businesses. Bad news: these small businesses used to be big businesses.
Today people are finding out that one can live as cheaply as two.

Business

Overheard at a shareholders' meeting: "Let's go. Whenever they fill in their speeches with little jokes, there isn't going to be a dividend."
He told me his company's products go all round the globe. I've just found out he makes lampshades.
The company is like one big happy family. Mainly because the boss hires all his relatives.

148

The boss told me, "This is just a suggestion. You don't have to follow it unless you want to keep your job."
It's an old firm. No Xerox, just a monk with a quill.

Cars

What I want is a new car with a warranty that lasts as long as the payments.
You can always tell an Italian car. They pinch your bottom.
It cost me $60 to have my car overhauled. I was speeding on the freeway when the police car overhauled it.
An old battered car travels the streets of Minneapolis carrying a sign that says, "Attention—winner in Twelve Crashes".
The conversation turned to: "What's the most frightening sound you can think of?" One said, "A groan in the dark when you think you're alone." Another said, "The slither of a black mamba in the grass." Finally the oldest of us growled, "I know a sound worse than all of yours put together. A long, low whistle coming from a mechanic underneath your car."

Charm

Charm is the ability to make somebody think both of you are pretty wonderful.
Charm is what everybody notices if you've got it and nobody notices if you haven't.

Children

Kids are a comfort in your old age—and they help you reach it faster as well.
It seems a shame that most parents weren't given their neighbors' children, because those are the only ones they know how to raise.
Children—they never put off till tomorrow what will keep them from going to bed tonight.
They should make great waiters when they grow up. They never come when you call them.
If you really want your kids to do what you say . . . say nothing.

Christmas

When the main difference between a man and a boy is the price of his toys.

It's that time when even the strongest of men get emotional over family ties—especially if they have to wear them.

When Cardinal O'Connor said there should be a religious message on Christmas stamps, *The New Yorker* suggested "Lord deliver us".

I feel strange using my credit card at Christmas—buying this year's gifts with next year's money.

Countryside

Consider the pitiful case of the fellow who wants to live in the country. He's moved out three times and each time the town has overtaken him.

A city boy spent his first night on the farm. The morning's activity woke him at four o'clock and he sat at breakfast half asleep and said, "It doesn't take long to stay here all night, does it?"

My four-year-old son coaxed Grandpa into letting him ride on the tractor during the ploughing. Later Grandma asked, "What were you doing in the field?" and he said. "I don't know whether we're taking the earth out or putting it back—but we're making it wider."

Criticism

If you want to avoid criticism, SAY NOTHING, DO NOTHING and BE NOTHING.

Never mind criticism. Most knocking is done by those who don't know how to ring the bell!

Cynicism

Instead of cursing the darkness, I lit one small candle and my fire insurance went up forty per cent.

My grandfather used to say, "If you keep your head above the surface, you can see the stars!" Mind you, he wasn't a philosopher ... he was a sewage worker.

There's only one sure way of reducing violence. Kill everybody.

There's only one way to grow old gracefully. You've got to die young.

Dance

I never dance on an empty stomach unless it's someone I don't like.

She came to the fancy dress ball completely nude except for a cross marked on each bosom. Said she was a chest of draws.

The difference between a cha-cha and pea-green paint is that anyone can learn to cha-cha.

We did the Politician's Polka—that's one step forward, two steps back, then you sidestep the issue, open your mouth and put your foot in it.

Death

We all have to go sometime. I usually go during the commercials.

Woody Allen said it: "I don't want to achieve immortality through my work. I want to achieve it through not dying!"

Debt

If you want to lose your shirt, keep putting too much on the cuff.

The thing that leads most people into debt, is trying to keep up with the people already there.

Definitions

Genius is a promontory jutting out into the future.

Contentment is the smother of invention.

A Yawn is Nature's way of letting a husband open his mouth.

Conscience is that small inner voice that warns you when somebody's watching.

Business is what, when you don't have any, you go out of.

Falsies: the bust that money can buy.
Incest: rolling your own.
Taxi Meter: device for showing you how fast you aren't getting there.
His: pronoun which means hers.
Ramparts: these are only of interest to a sheep.
Reunion: a lot of people getting together to see who's falling apart.
Optimist: a father who lets his teenage son borrow the car.
Pessimist: one who won't.
Pedestrian: one who did.

Diets

I'd have no objection to people who eat like sparrows if they'd only stop that everlasting chirping about it.
I'm on a food-free diet.
She's on a sea-food diet. Only has to see food and she eats it.
There's a new Chinese diet. Order all the food you want but use only one chopstick.
If you're thin, don't eat fast. And if you're fat, don't eat . . . *fast!*

Dirty

When an AMTRAK inspector made his annual visit to our local station, he was horrified by the dirt. He shouted, "Look at that ticket counter! The dust's so thick I could write my name in it." And our stationmaster said, "So you could, but don't forget, you're an educated man."
My friend says his wife's not houseproud: "We're probably the only family in our neighborhood with their Christmas decorations up all year round."

Disagreement

These days the only people who listen to both sides of an argument are the neighbors.
If you really want the last word in an argument, try saying, "I expect you're right."

Divorce

My wife would divorce me tomorrow if she could find a way to do it without making me happy.

My first wife was a clever housekeeper. When we divorced, she kept the house.

Divorce is too expensive. What I need is a wife transplant.

Dogs

"No wonder the collie is half asleep,
He earns his keep by counting sheep."

I've got a dog that barks all night for no reason. I'm thinking of buying him a burglar.

She said, "Rex is just like one of the family." And without thinking I said, "Really? Which one?"

Our dog has an ingrown tail. The only way I can find out if he's happy is to have him X-rayed.

Driving

The best safety device in a car is a rear-view mirror with a police car in it.

Drive carefully. The other guy's car may not be paid for either.

They say if you drink, don't drive. I don't even putt.

Be very careful parking. Accidents cause people.

My wife's driving is improving. Now she runs into cheaper cars.

Drunk

One of our town characters was dragged into (name of local town) Police Station, shouting, "What's the charge?" The sergeant said, "You were brought in for drinking." And the fellow said, "Oh, that's different—when do we start?"

I never knew my father drank till one night he came home sober.

They called my uncle "the town drunk"—which isn't so bad until you realize the town was Milwaukee.

I get dizzy after one drink. Usually the fifteenth.

153

He's a good health fanatic. Twenty times a day he says, "Good health!"

Why worry about tomorrow when today is so far off?

There's more to life than meets the mind.

Reality is just a figment of your imagination.

Easter

When I asked my 12-year-old son what he was going to give up for Lent, he said without hesitation, "My New Year's resolutions."

Spring is the time for all you younger guys to get at it and court—but don't get caught at it.

I spotted my first robin, and vice versa.

Economy

Funny word, "economy". It means the large size in coffee and the small size in cars.

Economy, The

I'm beginning to suspect God created the world as a tax loss.

Times are so hard that people who don't intend to pay aren't buying.

I phoned my stockbroker and Dial-a-Prayer answered.

The President knows it's serious. Sometimes he lies awake at work, worrying about it.

The Strong take it from the Weak and the Brainy take it from the Strong and the Government takes it from all of us.

Exaggeration

An exaggeration is only a truth that lost its temper.

Experience

For every man who speaks from experience there's a wife who isn't listening.

Faith

One person with a belief is equal to a force of ninety-nine who only have interests.
You can't do much with faith—and you can't do much without it.
Remember, nothing is impossible as long as you don't have to do it yourself.
Nothing's impossible, although I've never seen a worm that could fall over.

Fame

One thing's sure about stardom. It doesn't come in a twinkle.
Fame is when a madman thinks he's you.
Footprints in the sands of time aren't made by sitting down.

Fashions

Overheard in a dress shop: "My measurements are small, medium, and large—in that order."
Most husbands want their wives to wear their dresses longer—about two years longer.
I have firm ideas about my wife's clothes. I hate to see her in anything over twenty dollars.
Fashion news—no change in men's pockets this year.
Slits in women's skirts come in three different lengths—high, higher, and "Not guilty, your honor."

Friendship

Identify your friends by their enemies.

Gardening

Old gardeners never die—they just spade away.
Anyone who uses a power lawn mower before noon on Saturday should have to shave with it.
Remember—the family that rakes together, aches together.

I haven't got a green thumb. We've got a rock garden and last week three of them died.

Gifts

Ever since Eve gave Adam the apple there's been a misunderstanding between the sexes about gifts.

There are two kinds of people, the givers and the takers. The takers eat well. The givers sleep well.

Girls, Beautiful

I wouldn't trust her very far . . . and she wouldn't trust me very near.

She's the kind of girl you could take home to Mother . . . provided, of course, you can trust your father.

Men *do* make passes at girls who wear glasses . . . it all depends on their frames.

A lovely woman in a low-cut gown passed us and I said, "Now don't start entertaining evil thoughts." And (name) said, "I'm not, they're entertaining me."

Girls, In General

Why do girls who wear wigs, false eyelashes, and falsies always complain there are no real men any more?

The first thing I notice about an attractive woman is whether my wife is around.

Many a girl who says no expects to be held for further questioning.

She's a very quiet girl and she likes quiet things—like the folding of money.

She said. "I adore men who make things. How much do you make?"

156

Gossip

The woman who doesn't gossip has no friends to speak of.
Some people never get interested in anything until it's none of their business.
I hate to spread gossip, but what else can you do with it?
She can talk for two hours on what not to do if whatever might be doesn't happen.

Gratitude

Don't bite the hand that feeds you. There's more meat further up.
If your wife doesn't treat you as she should, be thankful.

Happiness

When you make two people happy, one of them is apt to be you.
You always know which people have found life a bed of roses; you hear them complaining about the thorns.
Robert Frost said happiness makes up in height what it lacks in length.
Happiness is a halfway station between too much and too little.

Health

Nobody is sicker than the man who is sick on his day off.
My doctor told me, "No more wine and women but sing all the songs you want."
You can tell how healthy a man is by what he takes two at a time—pills or stairs.
The picture of health requires a happy frame of mind.

Health Food

Glamor is an inside job.
Ah, there's nothing like wholesome cooking, and that's what my wife serves up—nothing like wholesome cooking.

157

Health foods are nothing new. When we were kids my mother served us health food ... if you knew what was good for your health, you ate the food.

Hippies

The hippie has gone the way of the American buffalo, to which he bore a strong resemblance.

History

If it's true that history repeats itself, where are those 1950 prices?
Nothing makes you feel your age more than discovering your children's history lessons are what you studied as current events.
Voltaire said it—history is nothing but a pack of tricks we play upon the dead.
And George Bernard Shaw said, "We learn from history that we learn nothing from history."

Horse-racing

You can still make a lot of money at the races, if you happen to be a horse.
You don't see me at the races throwing my money about. I've got a Government to support.
A horse is something that can run like hell until you bet twenty bucks he can.
The horse I bet on came in eighth but I was proud of him; it took seven other horses to beat him.
I bet on a horse that got a ticket for parking.

House and Home

Groucho Marx said, "Home is where you hang your head."
Ted Ray said home is the one place where whatever itches, you can scratch it.
There's no place like home, especially when you're looking for trouble.
Home: that's where he runs the show but she writes the script.

My neighbor has no civic pride. I swear his front lawn would never get cut if it weren't for my sheep.

Hunting

The judge said, "Why did you shoot at your hunting companion, Herr Merkel?" "I mistook him for a deer." "When did you note your error?" "When the deer shot back."

Paddy and Mick went hunting, saw a sign by the road: "BEAR LEFT", so they went home.

My uncle once followed some tracks into a cave and shot a train.

If your gun is loaded, you mustn't be.

My friend said, "I left it to you to bring all the provisions, and you bring a loaf of bread and seven bottles of booze. Now what the hell are we going to do with all that bread?"

Hurry

There are two things a man likes a woman to do in a hurry— dress and undress.

The man who hasn't time to waste on a red light always finds time to attend the funeral.

It's amazing how, when I haven't enough time to do a job properly, I always have enough time to do it over again.

Husbands

If there's one thing that makes a husband angrier than his wife refusing to tell him where the money went, it's her telling him.

Ladies, why is it the same husband who forgets your birthday never forgets your age?

He always knows the short cut that takes two hours longer.

But he doesn't trust his wife's driving until the kids have to be taken somewhere.

Husbands, let your wife know that you think about her occasionally . . . grind your teeth.

I'm what's known as a suburban husband. That's an oddjob man with occasional sex privileges.

Inspiration

Edward B. Newill, Vice President of General Motors, said this: "Let us recognize a basic truth. Success in life is not a destination. It is a journey. Fortunately, this means that no one is obliged to work toward a single distant goal and be judged successful only if he attains that one objective. As with a traveller, the end of the journey is usually beyond the range of vision, but there is much of interest and beauty along the way to reward each day's steps. The happiest journey is not made with downcast eyes which see only tired, dusty feet. It is made with uplifted sight to appreciate its significance and to picture what may lie beyond. The stars were made for those who look up and whose imagination knows no limitations."

When I'm feeling sorry for myself I simply go for a walk. And I keep right on walking and walking, looking around me as I go—at the front doors that hide other people's fears and joys, at the marvels of nature, at the courage and invention behind every church and factory, at the sheer size and complexity of the small part of the world my legs can cover—and if that doesn't make my worries seem insignificant by comparison, I get angry!

Insurance

My insurance man's asking far too much for the premium; last week he asked for it four times.

According to actuarial tables, people who live the longest are rich relatives.

An insurance agent is the only man who likes to see a girl fully covered.

Japan

Where else can a girl win a Beauty Contest and measure 18—12—18?

Ken Dodd says everything in Japan is miniaturized—and the women are none too pleased about it.

A full evening with a Japanese hostess comes to only $50; of course batteries are extra.

Jealousy

It's the blister of the heel of love.
Remember the man who didn't make love to his wife for ten years and then shot the man who did.
And the man on the flying trapeze who caught his wife in the act.
My first wife ran away with my best friend, whoever the hell he is.
Jealousy is a wife saying, "This seat belt's been tightened, who is she?"

Jewish

International authors were asked to write about elephants. The Englishman wrote, "The Elephant and How To Hunt It". The Italian wrote, "The Elephant and How To Cook It". The Frenchman wrote, "The Elephant and Sex". The German wrote 14 volumes called "The Elephant—An Introduction." And the Israeli distributed 500,000 leaflets headed "The Elephant and the Jewish Problem."
My friend is half Jewish and half Gypsy . . . what he can't buy wholesale, he steals.
Mrs. Cohen calls on a private detective: "I want you should follow my husband's mistress. I want to know in detail what she sees in him."

Kindness

The kindness planned for tomorrow doesn't count today.
Well, like they say, we're all in this world to help others. What I want to know is—what the hell are the others here for?

Kissing

Stealing a kiss sometimes leads to marriage, a perfect example of crime and punishment.
A kiss: something that brings two people so close together they can't see what's wrong with each other.

Knowledge

There's nothing as stupid as an educated man if you get him off the subject he was educated in.

Lateness

Rushing into the elevator, I bumped into my boss. He said, "Late again!" and I heard myself saying, "Yes, me too."

A teenage temp arrived late in my office and she said, "I'm sorry but a young man followed me from the bus stop." I said, "And that took you all this time?" And she said, "Well, he walked so slowly."

When I put my key in the front door I wonder what I'm letting myself in for.

Listen, if your wife no longer cares how late you come home, it's later than you think.

Law

My lawyer was attending a funeral. I arrived and took a seat beside him: "How far has the service gone?" He nodded toward the clergyman in the pulpit and whispered back, "He just opened the defense."

I sent my Counsel a message from the court, "Justice has prevailed." He wired back, "Appeal at once."

The prisoner said, "As God is my judge, I am innocent." The judge: "He's not, I am, and you're not."

It's easy to tell right from wrong. Wrong is more fun.

You've heard of Murphy's Law, and Parkinson's Law, but have you ever heard of Cole's Law? No? It's just shredded cabbage and mayonnaise.

Lazy

You can take the day off but you can't put it back.

In the space marked "Position Desired", one job applicant wrote, "Sitting".

(Name) will never be replaced by a computer. Where can you find a computer that does nothing?

He was off work again with his leg . . . the second leg of the Darts Match.
Laziness travels so slowly, poverty soon overtakes it.

Lies

The man who has never lied to the woman he loves probably has trouble communicating with members of the opposite sex.

Life

Life is like a shower. One wrong turn and you're in hot water.
Henry de Montherlant said. "The laws of life are founded on necessity, its charms on the non-essentials."
Life is like a taxi. The meter keeps running whether you're going anywhere or not.
If I had my life to live over again, I wouldn't have the strength.
Ah, the simple pleasures. They do your back no good but I like 'em.
A magazine once ran a competition for a statement of a philosophy of life that could be put on a postcard. The winner: "Love, trust, dare—and keep on doing it."
Life is like a cultivated mushroom. As soon as you put your head above the ground, someone heaps another load of fertilizer on it.

Losing your temper

Keep raising the roof and people will think there's something wrong in your attic.
Becoming thoroughly angry with people is often a stage in getting to know them. If we successfully pass this point and reach the stage of hilarious laughter, we have gone far in cementing friendship.

Love

Always remember the heart is only a muscle—so when you're in love, you're not really in love—you're muscle-bound.
Disraeli said it: "The magic of first love is our ignorance that it can ever end."
Love is blind. That's why you see so many spectacles in the park.
Love is the delusion that one man differs from another. (For men: "that one woman" ...)
Take love out of sex and all you're left with is X-Rated aerobics.

Luck

The luckiest man I know: his grandfather died, left him a fortune, he went to bury him and struck oil.
"I'm grateful for my bad luck. Without it, I could never explain my mistakes.
Sometimes a man doesn't know how lucky he is. I don't have that problem because my wife keeps telling me all day long.

Mankind

If you thought you were the only human being left on earth, how would you be sure? Do you know how? Get out a pack of cards and start playing a game of solitaire. If there's anyone else alive they'll be tapping you on the shoulder in a couple of minutes and saying, "That five goes on that six."
Man is put here to help man. Only a few months ago a friend of mine was having money trouble so, of course, I helped him out. He wept, he said, "I'll never forget you"—and he didn't. He's in trouble again and he just called me.

Marriage

It's an investment that pays dividends if you pay interest.
Or it's just another union that defies management.
A successful marriage involves falling in love many times—always with the same person.

164

A cynical friend of mine says, "Marrying a woman for her beauty is like buying a house for its paint."
A marriage counsellor I know ushers couples in with the words, "Think of my office as a demilitarized zone."
Marriage is a sort of graduation ceremony in which a man loses his Bachelor's Degree without acquiring a Master's.
If you've got half a mind to get married, that's all it takes.
When a husband's words are sharp, it may be from trying to get them in edgewise.

Medicine

Medical science has developed so amazingly in recent years that it's now almost impossible for a doctor to find anything about a patient that's all right.
We're born with medical assistance and most of us die the same way.
Every hospital has two kinds of patients . . . those who are ill and those who complain about the food.
A hospital notice: "Ring Bell Once If You Need Anything, Twice If It's Urgent, Three Times If It's Too Late."

Mediocrity

Only the mediocre are always at their best.

Meditation

My father taught me to meditate. He said, "Sit down and shut up!"
Sitting thinking the other night . . . it was late, TV was over, my wife had gone to bed and I was just sitting there finishing my nightcap . . . sewing the tassel on actually . . .
At least when you're not doing anything and you're *not* watching TV, you know you're not doing anything.

Memory

There is a difference between not thinking of someone and forgetting him.

I went to see a doctor about my failing memory. He made me pay in advance.

Women love nostalgia. My wife loves to delve into the past and say things like, "Where the hell were you last night?"

Middle Age

Middle age is when you get enough exercise just avoiding people who think you should have more.

You know you're middle-aged when the only thing you feel like exercising is caution.

When, instead of going on forty, you're going on Valium.

When you avoid going into antique shops in case someone makes an offer for you.

I admit it, I'm pushing fifty; got tired of pulling forty.

Modesty

It's easy to be humble when you're a success. The trick is to be arrogant when you're a flop.

Remember, a man is never so tall as when he stoops to shake hands with a chihuahua.

Money

Money in the bank is like toothpaste—easy to get it out, very hard to put it back.

The last time my wife borrowed money from me she said, "I'll pay you back on Friday when I get your pay envelope."

It's sad to see people squandering money and know you can't help them.

There are so many things more important than money. The trouble is, they all cost money.

Always borrow from a pessimist. He never expects to get it back.

Money is a constant worry. But our Government is working night and day to relieve us of this worry.

Narrow-minded

A puritan is somebody who never got over the embarrassing fact that he was born in bed with a woman.

She's so narrow-minded her ears touch.

He won't sleep with his wife because she's a married woman.

She won't let the dentist in her mouth until the third appointment.

Nature

Nature usually evens things up. A grasshopper is lazier than a bee but has better manners.

Pascal said it: "Nature is an infinite sphere whose center is everywhere and whose circumference is nowhere."

My brother says he's completely happy with the earth as his pillow and the sky as his blanket. He hasn't found peace of mind, he's lost his flat.

A hen is only an egg's way of making another egg.

Navy

My job aboard ship was to polish the brass. I had the shiniest captain in the fleet.

They found the *Titanic*. Now there's an Irish salvage crew out there searching for the iceberg.

She thinks a naval destroyer is a hula hoop with a nail in it.

Newspapers

Classified ad: "Local firm seeking attractive girl or woman with shorthand, typing and filing."

From an ad for a sale of postage stamps: "The British Empire will be disposed of in the morning, Southern Ireland remaining until after lunch."

New Year

My New Year's Eve couldn't have been duller if I were Adam.
New Year's Eve advice: Remember, if you drink, don't drive. And if you drive, don't park too close to the curb, I might be lying there.
I went to a Gay Nineties Party. All the men were gay and all the women were ninety.
Last New Year's Day, I felt as if I'd been using a trampoline in a ship's cabin.
Me and the Old Year usually pass out at the same time.

Office, The

I've never forgotten seeing three labels in a Government office: "URGENT", "FRANTIC" and "PASSING INTO LEGEND".
The Managing Director and I never disagree. He simply goes his way and I go his.

Originality

To be exactly the opposite is also a form of imitation.
Originality is rare. Most of us know a good thing as soon as the other fellow sees it.
My secretary has unique ideas but they're entirely confined to spelling.
Don't expect anything original from an echo.

Pain

It's the little things in life that hurt. You can sit on top of a mountain but you can't sit on top of a pin.

Parties

I like Zsa Zsa Gabor's remark: "I went to this gigantic party, darling, but it was so dull, I was the only one there I'd ever heard of."
Why is it that the ones who want to leave early and the ones who want to stay late are always married to each other?

I don't go to parties much. Only when I'm invited.

Perspective

Don't forget that to a switchboard operator you're nothing but a hole that occasionally has to be plugged.

Everything's relative. There's this man, 98 years old, and he broke a mirror. Now he's overjoyed that he's going to have seven years bad luck.

It's all in how you look at it. Dawn can be the beginning of a new day or the end of a big night!

Philosophy

My grandad left me with a great piece of philosophy. You can have money, lose money, you'll get new money. You can have love, lose love, you'll get new love. But if you lose your sense of humor, then you lose everything. In that respect, I can assure you that this audience has nothing to worry about.

I think I exist; therefore I exist, I *think*.

Today is the first day of the rest of your life . . . unless you're using a Hebrew calendar . . . then today is Sunday and tomorrow's Saturday.

It matters not if you let money slip through your fingers. Or even if you let love slip through your fingers. But if you let your fingers slip through your fingers, you're really in trouble.

Politics

Congressmen should always remember that they have to live with their consciences longer than they do with their constituents.

Politics makes estranged bedfellows.

It's been said that politics is the conduct of public affairs for private advantage. So don't avoid politics because it's full of hypocrites. There's always room for one more.

Truce is stranger than friction.

Pollution

You know you've got a pollution problem when you take a bath and the water leaves a ring round *you*.

There's only one sure way to get rid of toxic waste . . . disguise it as a radio-cassette player and leave it in an unlocked car in New York City.

Positive Thinking

In the words of one comedian: "Think positive, men! Say, 'I can and I will! I can and I will!'—and she'll say, 'You will if I let you! You will if I let you!'"

Cheer up! We may be worse off than we were yesterday, but we're better off than we'll be tomorrow.

Poverty

They say it's better to be poor and happy than rich and miserable. But couldn't something be worked out? Such as being moderately rich and just moody?

I was once so poor I used to buy a pint of milk for breakfast and a loaf of bread for lunch, and eat them for supper.

I wasn't born in a log cabin but my family moved into one as soon as they could afford it.

Being poor has its advantages. Your car keys, for instance, are never in your other trousers.

Prayers

Don't pray for lighter burdens, pray for stronger backs.
Sudden prayers make God jump.
Lord, grant the world patience. And I want mine now.

Prices

If you think the cost of living is high, try dying and see what it costs you.

Always be wary of the salesman who says you can't take it with you—because he's planning to take yours with him.

There's a bright side to inflation. I'm paying more in tax today than I ever dreamed of earning when I was young.

They say inflation's been beaten but I've never known a time when cheap was so expensive.

Proverbs

When in doubt, worry.

Do unto others as you would have them do unto you . . . unless you're a masochist.

The best things in life are free—as the Scotsman said when he stood over a baker's grating.

Love your enemies. It'll confuse the hell out of 'em.

Cast your bread upon the waters—but make sure the tide's coming in.

Make little things count. Teach arithmetic to dwarfs.

Punctuality

The trouble with being punctual is that no-one else is there to appreciate it.

The trouble with being punctual is that people think you have nothing better to do.

Punctuality is the art of guessing how late the other fellow's going to be.

Time is money. My, how time flies!

Questions

Why do missing teeth look so appealing in children and so unpleasant in us?

There are two sides to every question—so why is there only one answer?

Why is there such a difference between an event we can never forget and an event we will always remember?

A contestant won a quiz show tie-breaker on behavior. He was asked. "Where may a woman go without a man?" and replied, "Everywhere, except to the altar."

Ever notice how with some people, the more questions they ask, the fewer answers they remember?

Since time began, men have been asking that age-old question. And wives have been replying, "Not tonight, dear, I've got a headache."

Radio

Radio is a kind of television perfected to the point that only sound need be transmitted.

Speaking on radio for money is like joining a monastery to meet girls.

Rich

The futility of riches is stated very plainly in two places, the Bible and the income tax form.

A wealthy oil sheikh wrote his first letter to St Nicholas: "Dear Santa, If there's anything you want for Christmas, just ask."

There are two ways to get rich quick—marry money or divorce it.

He's so rich he has a parrot that says, "Polly wants a croissant." His answering machine has an answering machine. He hires Vidal Sassoon to cut his grass. Every morning he gets up and jogs for half a mile—from his bedroom to the kitchen.

Salesmanship

The customer greeted the salesman, "This message came for you." The salesman read it and groaned, "Oh no! My wife has presented me with twins." And the customer said, "Good, now you know how it feels to receive more goods than you order."

Is he good? He could sell Father's Day cards in a home for unwed mothers.

He could sell Michael Jackson two gloves.

School

My daughter's away at school for the first time. She wrote to her mother, "Please send me some stamps, they're so expensive here." What a great education system we have today. Those who can, do. Those who can't, teach. And those who can't teach, teach. Teachers today have their hands full. They have to hold chalk, a cane, a ruler, books, a loaded revolver.
Know why they call it corporal punishment? Because across your backside, you get two stripes.

Sex

Diamonds are a girl's best friend and a dog is a man's best friend. Now you know which sex has more sense.
Rhinoceros horn is supposed to be an aphrodisiac so I tried some. All I get is this occasional urge to charge at Land Rovers.
Remember, sex is not the answer. Sex is the question. *Yes* is the answer.
A woman shows her age first thing in the morning . . . a man last thing at night.
To go together is blessed. To come together is divine.
Woman lies to man. Man lies to woman. But the best part is when they lie together.
A great philosopher once said than men and women should put their differences behind them. Sounds either physically impossible or bloody agony.

Shopping

There are eight reasons why a woman buys something. Because—her husband says she can't have it, it will make her look young, it will make her look thin, her friends couldn't afford it, nobody has one, everybody has one, it's on special offer—and the eighth and most important reason of all—*because.*

173

My mother likes to shop in those large shopping malls. I've only just found out why. When she gets tired she can soak her feet in the fountain.

I became separated from my wife in (local department store) so I went up to an attractive salesgirl and said, "I don't want to buy anything. I'm just trying to find my wife and the minute I start talking to a pretty girl, she'll be here."

Short

Sir Gordon Richards was the first professional jockey to be knighted. He said, "Mother always told me my day was coming but I never realized I'd end up being the shortest knight of the year."

I just read that Danny DeVito had his pocket picked. Now that's what I call stooping low.

I try not to talk down to him but it isn't easy.

Show Biz

Comedian Fred Allen once said, "My agent gets ten per cent of everything I get, except my blinding headaches."

George Burns told Bob Hope it was time he retired. Hope said, "I'm 15 years younger than you. Why don't you retire?" Burns said, "I can't, I''m booked up."

An agent passed a building site and saw a man do five back somersaults and a head spin. He said, "I'll book you for the Palladium." The man said, "You'll have to book Bill as well. He's the one burned my backside with his blow-torch."

Signs

I saw it on our office noticeboard: "For sale, 1979 sports car, as new, price absurdly high, owner loves to haggle."

At our library entrance is a notice: "Welcome, Silent Majority."

On our computer room door it says, "Authorized Personnel Only. If You Have to Ask, You Aren't."

I rather liked the sign on a Xerox Company truck: "Please drive carefully, We can't duplicate *you*."

At my local garage a sign says, "We require a 50 per cent deposit from customers we don't know. And a 100 per cent deposit from some we do know."
In my local estate agents: "Buy Land—It's Not Being Made Any More."
In an antique shop: "There's No Present Like The Past."
In a jeweller's: Give her something to wrap around her little finger besides you."
On my accountant's wall: "There's no such thing as petty cash."
We have a local spiritualist who has a sign on her door: "Please ring bell. Knocking causes confusion."
In a furniture shop: "The best beds for love or money."
In a Dublin pub: "Never Drink on an Empty Pocket."

Silence

There's nothing wrong with having nothing to say as long as you don't insist on saying it.
You can tell when (name) has nothing to say. His lips move.
It's easier to suffer alone in silence if you're *positive* someone is watching.
To save face, keep lower half shut.
Silence is not only golden . . . it's seldom misquoted.

Sincerity

Remember these words. "Always be sincere . . . even if you don't mean it."

Smiles

I like to see a broad smile especially if she smiles at me.
If you want to drive your wife crazy, don't talk in your sleep, just smile.

Speeches

I love a finished speaker.
I really, truly do.
I don't mean one who's polished,
I just mean one who's through.
(Name) was in the middle of a speech when someone at the rear
shouted, "I can't hear you!"—and a man at the front yelled back,
"I'll change places with you!"
Speeches are like babies—easy to conceive but hard to deliver.

Success

The height of success in this world is having one's name written
everywhere . . . except in the telephone directory.
He's a success thanks to a combination of luck and pluck . . . the
luck of finding people to pluck.
I know an immigrant who came to this country only ten years
ago and already that man owes ¢980,000.
The recipe for success is the same as for a nervous breakdown!
Be nice to people on the way up—because you might get stuck
between floors and want to kill a little time.

Survival

Grandad had a long and hard life. I once asked him how he'd
made it through two World Wars, the Depression, and a lot of
other trials. He said, "The Bible, my boy. Time and again it says,
'And it came to pass'. But never once will you find it saying, 'And
it came to stay'."

Tax

This Tax Inspector saw a psychiatrist. He said, "I get the feeling
that the whole world hates me." The doctor said, "What nonsense,
the whole world doesn't hate you. The people of this country, yes,
but not the whole world."
I always put a dab of perfume on my tax return. Considering
what they're doing to me, I might as well get them in the mood.

I said to my Tax Inspector, "Have a heart!" He took it.

Teens

Teenagers are also parent agers.

My son and I have an almost Siamese Twin relationship. We're joined at the wallet.

He yelled at me, "I didn't ask to be born!" I yelled back, "Good thing you didn't—I'd have turned you down."

Television

Most of man's inventions have been time-savers . . . then came television.

As Johnny Carson has said, "The trouble with being a TV star is that you wind up in everyone's home but your own."

I once overheard a TV director saying to an actress, "More sincerity! This isn't just a line from some play, it's the commercial!"

I worry about all the time my children spend watching TV. My six-year-old only seems to know one word—"Sshhh!"

Invited to watch television, a very old lady up from the country said, "No thanks, I"ve already seen it."

Time

There's an old Irish proverb: God made time, but man made haste.

The banker's analysis of time: yesterday is a cancelled check, tomorrow is a promissory note, but today is cash—spend it wisely.

Time goes, you say? Ah no! Alas, time stays, we go.

Will Rogers said, "Half our life is spent trying to find something to do with the time we've rushed through life trying to save."

By the time you find greener pastures, you're too old to climb the fence.

Towns

When you return to your boyhood town, you find it wasn't the town you longed for. It was your boyhood.

Travel

I asked my travel agent when is the best time to go to Tahiti and he said, "Any time between 21 and 45."

I overheard two ladies: "Just came back from Mykonos." "Where's Mykonos?" "I don't know, we flew."

I get home so seldom that when I'm seen around the house, the neighbors gossip.

Troubles

Personally I always tell my troubles to my enemies. They are the only ones who really want to hear them.

Look out of the window from the breakfast table and you see the bird after the worm, the cat after the bird, and the dog after the cat. It gives you a little better understanding of the morning's news.

Truth

Remember Diogenes with his lamp searching for an honest man? Today he'd have to settle for a dishonest man who felt guilty about it.

The Greatest Lie of the 20th century: My vasectomy left no scar.

They say George Washington could never tell a lie. My wife can. As soon as she hears it.

Truth is hard to find. That's why I hardly believe anything I hear and only half of what I say. (Not that I ever lie, I just tell the truth creatively.)

Unemployment

When it comes to solving unemployment the Government just won't take *now* for an answer.

The Government's concerned with a working majority. They should do more to get a majority working.

There's one nice thing about not having a job. When you get up in the morning, you're already there.

178

Universities

I liked it the way it used to be, when student bodies were only interested in other student bodies.

Value

Never tell a woman you're unworthy of her love. She knows. How much would you be worth if you lost all your money?

War

Herodotus said it: "In peace, sons bury their fathers. In war, fathers bury their sons."
World War Three is unique because it will never be mentioned in history books.

Waste

Nothing is more wasted than a smile on the face of a slender girl with a 40-inch bust.

Weather

There's one good thing about snow . . . it makes my garden look just as nice as my neighbor's.
My doctor advised me to walk more and I've learned something—bad weather always looks much worse through a window.
My grandfather used to say no matter how bad the weather is, it's better than none at all. I never did understand that man.

Wedding Anniversary

To ensure the success of our dinner party, I made all the arrangements including an iced layer cake with the inscription "YOU ARE MY ONE AND ONLY" and I asked the caterers to make it a great big "ONE". When the cake was brought in I had the delicate task of explaining to my wife, who is sensitive about her weight, why the inscription read. "TO MY GREAT BIG ONE AND ONLY".

My wife gave me something I always wanted . . . she let me win an argument.

A Crystal Anniversary: 15 years of my wife being able to see right through me.

A Paper Anniversary: 10 years of coming home to find a note saying my dinner's in the oven.

Winning

A great philosopher once said, "Nice guys finish last." Or was it a great nymphomaniac?

Wives

The ideal wife is one who remains faithful to you but tries to be just as agreeable as if she weren't.

The wife who insists on wearing the trousers usually finds some other woman is wearing the mink.

When your wife asks to see something more expensive, she's shopping. When she asks to see something cheaper, she's buying.

Wives are smarter . . . they never marry a man for his big boobs.

Work

The 40-hour week has no charm for me. I'm looking for the 40-hour day.

Quite a few people are already working a 4-day week. Trouble is it takes them five or six days to do it.

If you've got to work for an idiot, you might as well work for yourself.

Pitch in and do your part. Some day we won't have a part to pitch in.

World, The

One problem with the world is that so many people who stand up vigorously for their rights fall down miserably on their duties.

If we want to make a new world we certainly have the material ready . . . first one was made out of chaos.

My eight-year-old was writing busily and she told me, "I'm writing an essay on the world." "That's a pretty tall order." "Not really, three of us in my class are working on it."

The world is full of willing people. Half willing to work, the rest willing to let them.

Yawns

If you happen to yawn while I'm speaking, I won't mind. A yawn is Nature's way of letting married men open their mouths.

I can't stop yawning. They put me on a course of iron tablets and I came down with metal fatigue.

Youth

Youth calls to youth, which is as it should be . . . but it probably explains why the rest of us can't get to the the phone.

Special Occasions

LINES FOR A WEDDING SPEECH

Straight away I want to refute the vicious rumor that's been going around here today that the bride and groom *had* to get married. That's a wicked lie. They could easily have waited another couple weeks.

Although I do hope the bride is expecting a little one. Otherwise she's going to be disappointed tonight.

(NB: Don't use either of those lines unless you're certain that the crowd is broadminded and the bride isn't pregnant.)

I've already congratulated the groom, I said, "Old pal, you will always look back on this day as the happiest of your life." This was yesterday.

This marriage will last a lifetime and that's unusual these days. I know a couple who broke up before their wedding pictures were developed. And they were Polaroid.

Traditionally June is supposed to be the month for weddings. This year alone, if all the June honeymoon couples were put end to end, they'd be doing it all wrong.

It was a beautiful ceremony. I found it very moving to see my old pal taking his two marriage vows—Silence and Poverty.

But our lovely bride has always said she wanted a very simple wedding and that's what she got—starting with the groom.

There are some wonderful wedding presents—toasters and saucepans—I hope he likes boiled toast.

I sent my wedding present last week and I've already received a charming thank-you note from the bride to say it was just what she wanted and she'd use them every time she entertained friends. Now I'm worried. I gave her bedsheets.

I gave the groom a book called *The Joy of Sex*. I thought he could take it on the honeymoon and read it during his off moments.

I've been worried for the groom ever since that moment at the altar. The rest of you weren't close enough to hear this—but when the clergyman said, "You may kiss the bride," she said, "Not now, I've got a headache."

What advice can I give our newlyweds from my vast store of experience and wisdom? Well, for one thing, be sure to keep your Marriage License in a very safe place because it's one of the most important documents you will ever have. You can't get a divorce without it.

Advice to the groom? Easy. When she hands you a dishcloth, blow your nose on it and hand it back.

To the father of the bride I can only say this. You're not losing a daughter, you're gaining a bathroom.

In the words of the song, you've "only just begun". There are bound to be a few little mistakes in a new marriage. Remember the newly-wed couple who didn't know the difference between putty and vaseline? A week later all their windows fell out. Which was the least of their worries.

None of the married men here will ever forget their wedding nights. Pajamas under the pillow in case there's a fire. And your bride coming shyly from the bathroom, all coy and cute in her new nightie, her hair falling softly around her perfumed shoulders, a vision of feminine beauty and desire. Next morning she's up early before you wake up to put on her make-up for breakfast . . .

Give it six months. She flops into bed in curlers, half a pound of grease on her face, dressed for an army assault course. She comes to the breakfast table looking as if she came second in a suicide contest. And if the doorbell rings she says, "You go. I can't let the milkman see me like this!"

It's important to establish the ground rules early in a marriage. My dad did that. Just as soon as they'd arrived in the bridal suite, he took his trousers off, tossed them to his bride and said, "Put 'em on!" My mom gave him a funny look but she put them on and said, "Well?" He said, "That, my dear, is the first and last time you wear the trousers in this marriage." She took his trousers off, pulled off her knickers and threw then at him. She said, "Put *them* on!" He said, "I'll never get into *them*!" She said, "No, and until you change your attitude, sweetheart, you won't!"

JEWISH GATHERINGS

"In our religion," explained a great Jewish actor in a speech, "the sin of eating bread on Passover is comparable to committing adultery. I told this to your Chairman and he tells me he's tried them both and can't see the comparison."

The actor's advice to me was a little more practical: "To an audience that's one hundred per cent Jewish, you can get away with almost any good Yiddish story. But with a large percentage of non-Jewish people present, even the best of those jokes can sound racist. So play it safe. Only use a tale that pokes affectionate or respectful fun at God's Chosen." And he gave me these lovely examples:

They named a Jewish holiday after my sex life . . . Passover.

Two little boys are talking: "Hey, Manny, what's nine and five?" Manny says, "Are you buying or selling?"

He plays orthodox golf. Never drives on Saturday.

Goldblum is knocked down by a car. A passerby puts his coat under Goldblum's head and asks, "Are you comfortable?" Goldblum says, "Listen, I make a living."

What's a Jewish grandmother's favorite nine-letter word? "Eateateat!"

I know a dentist with such a huge respect for religion, he treated a clergyman and refused the fee. And that clergyman was so grateful, he sent the dentist a Bible as a gift. Another time, a Catholic priest came to him for treatment, again he refused payment and the priest sent him a silver crucifix. Soon after that, a rabbi came in for dental work, the dentist refused payment and the rabbi sent him another rabbi.

LAUGHING ON RELIGIOUS GROUNDS

Every comedian has a few gags about religion in his repertoire and most churchmen have even more. I've yet to attend a function with a member of the clergy present where a good-natured joke about his calling didn't win a warm wave of laughter. You may be called upon to "say a few words" at just such an occasion, a christening party perhaps, or a church fund-raising effort. Here are four favorites of other comedians, and a collection of my own.

Les Dawson tells the one about his clergyman leaving their parish after thirty years. "My wife said, 'I'm sorry to see you go, sir, because before you came to this neighborhood we didn't know what sin was.'"

185

Woody Allen declared, "There is no God. And furthermore, try getting a plumber on a weekend."

One of my friends knows a man of mixed parentage and religious loyalties, being part Muslim, part Hebrew and part Catholic. Three times a day he kneels towards Mecca and sings, "Oy Vay Maria".

Jerry Stevens says, "Us Italian Catholics nearly had an Irish Pope, but the Vatican changed the decision at the last minute. They found out the first thing he was going to do was wallpaper the Sistine Chapel."

Before coming here today I popped into the church, dropped $10 in the poor box and asked the reverend to bless my speech. He read it, gave me back the $10 and dropped my speech in the poor box.

I saw a minister wearing a T-shirt that said "CLERGYMEN DO IT WITH FAITH". That wouldn't have been so bad, but beside him was a girl wearing one that said, "I'M FAITH."

There's nothing like being honest with yourself and with your God. It's not always so easy being completely truthful to your minister. A woman moved into a new house near us and the reverend called. He said, "Are you a churchgoer?" She said, "Every Sunday to every service, sir, until my legs wouldn't allow it. Now I just have to worship in my own way at home." He said, "I see, you study the Good Book?" She said, "Constantly, all day and every day." Then she called to her little girl, "Tracey, go and fetch that big thick book that mommy's always reading." And the kid came back with a Sears catalogue.

Two nuns took a stroll through the woods at twilight, two men leapt out of the bushes, ripped off the nuns' habits and had their wicked way with them. Sister Maria, shaken and shocked, looked up to heaven and cried, "Forgive them, Lord, they know not what they do." And Sister Kathleen looked over and said, "Mine does."

When you pause to think about what God created—the heavens, the earth, the mountains and valleys, the birds of the air and the beasts of the forest, and it only took Him six days. Fantastic! Only six days. It took the landlord six months to put a new toilet in my mother's bathroom. And that's not all—after God made the earth, he flooded it. And the same thing happened to my mother's bathroom.

Our old bishop used to say that church members are either pillars or caterpillars. The pillars hold up the church, the caterpillars just crawl in and out.

I've devoted my life to relieving morally handicapped women.

Our minister said, "Any person in this church who has committed adultery without shame, let him stand up." So I stood up. He said, "Are you without shame?" I said "No, but I didn't like to see you standing up by yourself."

God doesn't pay his workers large salaries—but the retirement benefits are out of this world.

My wife is a good Catholic. In fact she's such a good Catholic we can't get fire insurance—too many candles in the house.

There's always been a degree of prejudice in every religion. A Reverend saw this little Asian lad walking into his church so he whispered, "Hey you! This is a white Protestant church, not some heathen pagan temple of six-armed demons! Go away and pray to Almighty God in Heaven for guidance!"

Next day the little Asian lad came back. He said, "Mister, I prayed to Almighty God just like you said and while I was on my knees, the Lord spoke to me." "And just what would the Almighty have to say to someone like you?" The Asian boy said, "Sir, the Lord is saying to me, 'Gupta, what are you praying for down there?' And I am saying, 'Lord, I am wishing to go into Mr. Paisley's church.' And the Lord, he is laughing and laughing and saying, 'Sonny, you have no chance—I've been trying to get in there for twenty years myself.'"

There seems to be some new religion or other springing up every day. I heard of a weird one just this morning—the Orthodox Civil Servants. They believe that when you die your soul goes to Washington where it gets lost in all the paperwork.

I've only attended one ecumenical conference and some of the debates spilled over into the dining areas. At one table an earnest young Catholic priest and an equally emphatic Episcopalian minister were arguing fiercely about whose religion was the true one. A wise old rabbi listened a while, then said, "You are both very sincere men of the cloth, but after all, we're all working for God. All I can suggest to you is this—you two go on teaching His laws in *your* ways and I'll go on teaching His laws in *His*."

Not being a Catholic, the only two words I know in Latin are "Rhythm and Blues." You use the rhythm method and when it doesn't work, you get the blues.

It's easy enough for me to stand here handing out advice. The test of it is whether or not I'd take it myself. Remember the classic story of the carpenter working in a church when he hits his thumb an almighty thump and yells, " *Hell!*" The priest hears him, rushes over and says, "Bob, when you hurt yourself, don't curse like that. Swearing is the very sound of evil itself. If you're in pain, instead of blasphemy and profanity just say, 'Help me, Lord' and the Lord will help you." Bob says, "But I split me thumb and it's bleeding and I think I broke it, father—*oh hell!*" The priest says, "Stop that now! What have I just been telling you?" Bob says, "Yes father, all right, I'll do like you say—*Help me Lord!*" A shaft of light beams down from heaven, an angel choir sings, Bob's thumb stops bleeding, the bone knits, the skin heals up—and the priest says, "*oh hell!*"

Religious faith has a lot to do with your perspective. One goldfish said to the other goldfish. "Do you believe in God?" And the other goldfish said, "Of course I do, who do you think changes the water?"

It's amazing how easy it is to say the wrong thing in public unintentionally. Our church treasurer, Mr. Greenhill, ran off with all the funds. Our minister stood up in the pulpit and said, "I am very sorry to have to tell you that our church treasurer, Mr. Greenhill, has absconded with all the funds. We shall now sing hymn number 406, 'There is a green hill far away.'"

I love watching faithhealers on television. There's an elderly couple sitting listening to the Reverend Jimmy Swaggart asking for donations and he's saying, "All you people out there in televisionland, with the Lord's help I want to heal you! Put one hand on the television and your other hand on the part that needs healing and have faith!" The old lady puts one hand on the television and the other on her heart. The old man puts one hand on the television and the other in his lap. And the old lady says, "No, George, the preacher said heal the sick, not raise the dead."

Some of you may remember a famous bandleader of the dance band days named Roy Fox. Roy had a brother who was a Roman Catholic priest and Roy loved to tell the story of how his brother was not wearing his priest's collar when a cop stopped him for speeding. The priest said, "I'm Father Fox." And the cop said, "I don't care if you're Mother Goose, you're still getting a ticket."

THE FINAL WORD No matter how well you think you're doing, there's always the possibility that the man at the top will see it another way. Take the classic tale of Sergio who drops his toast and it falls on the floor with the butter and jam side *upwards!* He rushes to the priest, tells him what happened and says. "Father, would the Church confirm that I've been blessed with an Official Miracle?" The priest thinks to himself, "Well, Sergio always puts all his change in the collection box, I'll check it out," so he goes to the Cardinal. The Cardinal goes to the Pope and says, "Your Holiness, one of our devoted brethren has a member of his flock who dropped his toast and it fell on the floor with butter and jam side upwards. He wants to know—is it a miracle? What shall we tell him?" And the Pope said, "Tell him he buttered the wrong side."

The final word is really yours, of course, because this book is no more than a motorist's manual. How you drive is up to you. And if I just happen to be in the audience the next time you speak, give me a wink. I promise to laugh the loudest in all the right places. I wish you the best of luck and, in Oscar Hammerstein II's famous song title, "Happy Talk"!